DREAMSCAPES: A MYSTICAL ANALYSIS OF DREAM SYMBOLS

Integrating Dreamwork into
Spiritual Practices

D.R. T STEPHENS

S.D.N Publishing

Copyright © 2023 S.D.N Publishing

All rights reserved

The characters and events portrayed in this book are fictitious. Any similarity to real persons, living or dead, is coincidental and not intended by the author.

No part of this book may be reproduced, or stored in a retrieval system, or transmitted in any form or by any means, electronic, mechanical, photocopying, recording, or otherwise, without express written permission of the publisher.

ISBN: 9798865847373

CONTENTS

Title Page
Copyright
General Disclaimer   1
Chapter 1: A Friendly Welcome to the Mystical World of Dreams   3
Chapter 2: The Universal Language of Dreams   6
Chapter 3: The History of Dream Interpretation   9
Chapter 4: The Psychology of Dreaming   13
Chapter 5: Types of Dreams and Their Meaning   17
Chapter 6: Decoding Dream Symbols   20
Chapter 7: Dream Journals: Your Personal Oracle   24
Chapter 8: Dreaming and the Chakra System   28
Chapter 9: Cultural Contexts of Dream Interpretation   32
Chapter 10: The Scientific Perspective on Dreams   35
Chapter 11: Dream Imagery and Archetypes   38
Chapter 12: Animal Totems and Dream Symbolism   42
Chapter 13: Dream Symbols in Literature and Mythology   45
Chapter 14: Ethics of Dream Interpretation   48
Chapter 15: A Practical Guide to Beginner Dreamwork   52
Chapter 16: Advanced Dream Journaling Techniques   56
Chapter 17: Dreams and Altered States of Consciousness   60

Chapter	Title	Page
Chapter 18	Synchronicities: The Role of Dreams in Daily Life	63
Chapter 19	Dream Incubation Techniques	67
Chapter 20	Nightmares and Shadow Work	71
Chapter 21	Dreams and Astral Projection	74
Chapter 22	The Kabbalistic Approach to Dream Interpretation	78
Chapter 23	Dream Yoga and Tibetan Practices	81
Chapter 24	Dreams and Divination	85
Chapter 25	Dream Symbols in Sacred Geometry	88
Chapter 26	Dreams and the Cycle of Life: Birth, Death, Rebirth	91
Chapter 27	Dream Telepathy and Shared Dreaming	94
Chapter 28	Dreams in the Alchemical Tradition	97
Chapter 29	Interpreting Paradoxical and Illogical Dream Elements	101
Chapter 30	Sleep Disorders and Their Impact on Dreaming	105
Chapter 31	Quantum Dreaming: The Frontiers of Dream Science	109
Chapter 32	Lucid Dreaming as a Spiritual Practice	113
Chapter 33	Time and Dreams: The Temporal Dimension	117
Chapter 34	The Shamanic Journey: Dreams as Spiritual Quests	120
Chapter 35	Archetypal Patterns and Cosmic Symbols	123
Chapter 36	Dream Interpretation in Transpersonal Psychology	127
Chapter 37	Analyzing Recurring Dream Themes	131
Chapter 38	Dreams, Déjà Vu, and Anomalies of Consciousness	135

Chapter 39: Activating the Third Eye Through Dreamwork	138
Chapter 40: Sacred Dream Circles: Collective Dream Interpretation	142
Chapter 41: Erotic Dreams and Spiritual Alchemy	146
Chapter 42: Dream Mapping: Advanced Symbol Networks	149
Chapter 43: Transcending the Self: Non-Dual Awareness in Dreaming	152
Chapter 44: Integrating Dream Wisdom into Daily Spiritual Practice	156
Chapter 45: A Positive Farewell: The Infinite Possibilities of Dreamwork	159
THE END	163

GENERAL DISCLAIMER

This book is intended to provide informative and educational material on the subject matter covered. The author(s), publisher, and any affiliated parties make no representations or warranties with respect to the accuracy, applicability, completeness, or suitability of the contents herein and specifically disclaim any implied warranties of merchantability or fitness for a particular purpose.

The information contained in this book is for general information purposes only and is not intended to serve as legal, medical, financial, or any other form of professional advice. Readers should consult with appropriate professionals before making any decisions based on the information provided. Neither the author(s) nor the publisher shall be held responsible or liable for any loss, damage, injury, claim, or otherwise, whether direct or indirect, consequential, or incidental, that may occur as a result of applying or misinterpreting the information in this book.

This book may contain references to third-party websites, products, or services. Such references do not constitute an endorsement or recommendation, and the author(s) and publisher are not responsible for any outcomes related to these third-party references.

In no event shall the author(s), publisher, or any affiliated parties be liable for any direct, indirect, punitive, special, incidental, or other consequential damages arising directly or indirectly from any use of this material, which is provided "as is," and without warranties of any kind, express or implied.

By reading this book, you acknowledge and agree that you assume all risks and responsibilities concerning the applicability and consequences of the information provided. You also agree to indemnify, defend, and hold harmless the author(s), publisher, and any affiliated parties from any and all liabilities, claims, demands, actions, and causes of action whatsoever, whether or not foreseeable, that may arise from using or misusing the information contained in this book.

Although every effort has been made to ensure the accuracy of the information in this book as of the date of publication, the landscape of the subject matter covered is continuously evolving. Therefore, the author(s) and publisher expressly disclaim responsibility for any errors or omissions and reserve the right to update, alter, or revise the content without prior notice.

By continuing to read this book, you agree to be bound by the terms and conditions stated in this disclaimer. If you do not agree with these terms, it is your responsibility to discontinue use of this book immediately.

CHAPTER 1: A FRIENDLY WELCOME TO THE MYSTICAL WORLD OF DREAMS

Welcome, dream voyagers and spiritual seekers, to a mystical journey where waking life and dreamscapes intermingle, offering a tapestry of symbols, messages, and experiences. Dreams have long captivated the human imagination, filling our nights with mystery and offering gateways to other dimensions of existence. But what is it about dreams that make them so intriguing, so fascinating? What gifts lie dormant in the enigmatic visuals, the obscure narratives, and the ever-changing landscapes of our nocturnal adventures? This book, "Dreamscapes: A Mystical Analysis of Dream Symbols," seeks to answer these questions and more as it delves into the rich world of dream interpretation and its integration into spiritual practices.

The Significance of Dreams

Dreams aren't just random concoctions of the sleeping brain; they offer a glimpse into the subconscious mind—a wondrous realm where emotional patterns, unfulfilled desires, and life insights reside. In religious texts and mystical traditions, dreams have often been seen as divine messages or spiritual experiences. In the Christian tradition, dreams like Joseph's served as prophetic insights. Islamic beliefs hold that dreams can come from Allah as a form of guidance. Likewise, shamans in various cultures view dreaming as a type of soul journey, while Eastern philosophies such as Hinduism and Buddhism see the dream state as an alternate reality, different yet deeply interconnected with our waking state.

The Bridge Between Dreams and Spirituality

Integrating dreamwork into spiritual practices can be a transformative experience. The symbolic nature of dreams serves as a profound tool for self-investigation, providing signs and metaphors that resonate with your spiritual quest. Many esoteric and mystical traditions provide frameworks for understanding these symbols in a deeper context. By combining a spiritual lens with the examination of your dreams, you can unveil layers of meaning and wisdom that enrich your waking life and spiritual journey.

For instance, if you are someone who practices mindfulness or meditation, you'll find that dream recall can become more vivid, and the symbols in your dreams can carry significant messages concerning your spiritual path. They might confirm that you're on the right track, or they could offer clues to unexplored territories of your inner world. These symbols often appear as common archetypes, animal totems, or even sacred geometry. In fact, the same symbols can recur across various mystical traditions, indicating a sort of universal language of the soul that is tapped into through dreams.

How This Book Will Guide You

"Dreamscapes: A Mystical Analysis of Dream Symbols" is

designed to be your comprehensive guide through this intricate and fascinating realm. The initial chapters will provide you with essential basics—how to understand the language of dreams, the psychology behind them, and their historical interpretations across various cultures. As you move into the intermediate sections, you'll encounter more specific methods for dream interpretation, different types of dreams, and their relations to altered states of consciousness. Finally, the advanced chapters will immerse you into the profound depths of mystical dream analysis, involving quantum theory, transpersonal psychology, and even spiritual alchemy.

This multi-layered approach ensures that whether you are a beginner who has just started pondering the mysteries of dreams, or an experienced dream analyst, there is something valuable for you in this book. By traversing through these pages, you'll gain a comprehensive understanding of the many aspects of dreams, from the straightforward to the enigmatic.

To begin your exploration, it is encouraged to keep an open mind and a willing spirit. This realm is one of boundless imagination and unlimited potential, where your willingness to engage directly impacts the richness of the experience.

Now, prepare to dive into this captivating subject, as each chapter opens a new door, offering perspectives and tools to decode the mysterious landscapes of your dreams. So keep your dream journal at hand as you embark on this enlightening journey; you never know what treasures you might uncover in the depths of your dreamworld.

CHAPTER 2: THE UNIVERSAL LANGUAGE OF DREAMS

Dreams have captivated human interest for millennia, serving as windows into the subconscious mind. They are universal experiences, yet they often come shrouded in a complex tapestry of symbols and emotions that defy straightforward interpretation. Unraveling the meaning behind these symbols is akin to learning a new language—the universal language of dreams. This chapter delves into the fundamental concepts and theories surrounding this intriguing form of communication between the conscious and the unconscious mind.

The Psychoanalytic Tradition: Freud and Jung

Sigmund Freud and Carl Jung are seminal figures in understanding dreams as a form of language. Freud's theory centered around the idea that dreams act as the "royal road to the unconscious." He posited that dream symbols were primarily sexual in nature and that they served as a safety valve for repressed desires. For Freud, the manifest content—the actual events of the dream—was less important than the latent content—the hidden psychological meaning. His method of dream analysis often involved free association, where an individual would say whatever came to mind in relation to a dream symbol, to unearth its subconscious implications.

Jung, a one-time student of Freud, diverged from his teacher in significant ways. He posited that dreams not only reveal personal unconscious content but also tap into a collective unconscious shared by all of humanity. According to Jung, this collective unconscious contains archetypes—universal symbols like the Hero, the Mother, or the Wise Old Man—that recur across cultures and time periods. Jung believed that dreams aimed at achieving individuation, a process of becoming the person one is inherently meant to be. His approach to dream interpretation involved not just associating symbols with personal experiences, but also relating them to universal archetypes.

Cognitive and Neuroscientific Perspectives

Modern cognitive psychology and neuroscience offer a different lens through which to view the language of dreams. Cognitive theories often focus on problem-solving and memory consolidation as core functions of dreaming. According to the activation-synthesis hypothesis, a model from neurobiology, dreaming is essentially a byproduct of neural activity during sleep. Brain regions responsible for emotions and memories become activated, and the cortex tries to synthesize or make sense of this activity by weaving it into a narrative. While this explanation may seem to demystify dreams, it doesn't negate the importance of symbols. Even if dreams originate from neural firings, the brain's attempt to synthesize these into coherent narratives gives rise to symbolic content that can still hold personal or universal meaning.

Cultural and Spiritual Interpretations

Understanding the language of dreams is not confined to psychoanalytic or scientific perspectives. Many indigenous cultures around the world view dreams as a form of spiritual communication. In some Native American traditions, dreams are considered messages from the spirit world and a medium through which one gains wisdom, healing, or even prophetic insights. Similarly, in Eastern philosophies, dreams are often seen as an extension of one's spiritual journey. In Islamic tradition, for instance, dreams hold a significant place, believed to be a source of divine guidance.

These cultural and spiritual perspectives, while different in their focus, underscore the universality of dreams as a form of language that transcends linguistic, cultural, and temporal barriers. They show that dreams have been, and continue to be, interpreted as meaningful across diverse frameworks, further solidifying their status as a universal language.

Summary

The language of dreams is complex and multifaceted, inviting interpretation from various angles—be it psychoanalytic theories of Freud and Jung, modern scientific models, or spiritual and cultural perspectives. Regardless of the lens through which one chooses to view dreams, they remain a form of communication that taps into deeper layers of the human mind, offering valuable insights into our inner workings. As we move through this book, we will delve deeper into the intricacies of interpreting this universal language, equipping you with the tools to understand your dreams and, by extension, yourself.

CHAPTER 3: THE HISTORY OF DREAM INTERPRETATION

Dreams have fascinated humans for millennia, serving as mirrors to our subconscious and portals to alternate realities. This chapter will delve into the rich tapestry of dream interpretation across various cultures and eras. Understanding the historical context of dream interpretation can provide a multifaceted lens through which we can more deeply comprehend our own dream experiences.

Ancient Civilizations and Dream Oracles

In ancient civilizations, dreams were often seen as prophetic messages from the divine. The Greeks, for example, had dedicated temples for dream incubation, where individuals would sleep in sacred spaces with the hope of receiving guidance in their dreams. The priests and priestesses at these temples would interpret the dreams and offer advice based on them.

Mesopotamian cultures also had a strong tradition of dream interpretation, as evidenced by ancient cuneiform texts that contain dream dictionaries. These texts offered interpretations for various dream symbols and were used by priests to guide kings and nobility in their decision-making. The Egyptian "Dream Book," a papyrus document dating back to the 13th century BCE, also outlines interpretations of dreams, ranging from ominous warnings to favorable omens.

The Judeo-Christian Tradition

In Judeo-Christian traditions, dreams have a significant place both in the Bible and in later religious teachings. Biblical figures like Joseph and Daniel were esteemed dream interpreters whose skills were believed to be gifts from God. In both cases, dreams were perceived as vehicles for divine messages that could influence the course of history. Joseph's interpretation of Pharaoh's dream about seven fat and seven lean cows, for example, led to preparations for a seven-year famine, ultimately saving countless lives.

In Christian monastic traditions, dreams were seen in a more complex light. While some monks and theologians considered dreams as potential divine revelations, others warned that they could be the work of the devil, intending to mislead and deceive. This dual perspective influenced Christian thought and created a nuanced, if somewhat ambivalent, view of dreams and their significance.

Eastern Philosophies and Dreamwork

In Eastern philosophies such as Hinduism and Buddhism, dreams are considered to be a reflection of the inner workings of the mind and are linked to the concept of Maya, or the illusionary nature of reality. In Tibetan Buddhism, the practice of Dream Yoga incorporates lucid dreaming as a path toward enlightenment. These philosophies often diverge from Western viewpoints by emphasizing the dreamer's ability to control and learn from the dream state rather than viewing dreams as external messages to be deciphered.

In Hinduism, dreams are classified into different categories, such as dreams related to the physical body, the emotional mind, and the deeper soul. Each category of dreams serves as a different channel for self-awareness and spiritual development. The Indian epic, the Mahabharata, even contains stories where dreams serve as allegorical devices for moral and philosophical teachings.

Modern Psychological Approaches

The Enlightenment era and the rise of scientific skepticism led to a decline in the view of dreams as divine or mystical messages. However, the emergence of psychology as a scientific discipline in the 20th century brought new perspectives on dream interpretation. Sigmund Freud's "The Interpretation of Dreams" argued that dreams were a window into the unconscious mind, replete with suppressed desires and conflicts. Carl Jung, a student of Freud, expanded upon this by introducing the concept of archetypes and the collective unconscious, further enriching the landscape of dream interpretation.

In more recent times, cognitive psychology and neuroscience have contributed to the understanding of dreams by exploring the neural mechanisms and cognitive processes that occur during sleep. However, despite the advancements in scientific understanding, dreams continue to be a subject of fascination, mystery, and spiritual exploration, weaving a complex narrative that bridges the empirical and the mystical.

Summary

The history of dream interpretation is a compelling journey across cultures and time, from ancient oracles to modern psychology. This rich heritage not only serves as a backdrop for contemporary dreamwork but also enriches our understanding of dreams as multi-dimensional phenomena that continue to captivate and inspire. As we delve deeper into the various theories and techniques surrounding dream interpretation in subsequent chapters, this historical context provides a foundational understanding that adds depth and nuance to the tapestry of dream exploration.

CHAPTER 4: THE PSYCHOLOGY OF DREAMING

Introduction

Dreams have intrigued humanity for millennia, not just as a mysterious phenomenon occurring during sleep, but also for their enigmatic symbolism and narrative structures. While religious texts and philosophical treatises have attempted to explore the meanings behind dreams, psychology has offered its own empirically-grounded perspective on why we dream and what those dreams might signify. This chapter delves into some of the foundational psychological theories surrounding dreams, beginning with the groundbreaking work of Sigmund Freud and progressing to Carl Jung's archetypal interpretations.

Sigmund Freud and the Psychoanalytic Perspective

Sigmund Freud, often dubbed the father of psychoanalysis, was among the first to offer a psychological framework for understanding dreams. Freud believed that dreams were a "royal road" to the unconscious mind. According to Freud, our unconscious desires and thoughts, often repressed due to societal norms or moral concerns, find a way to surface during sleep. These manifest in the form of dreams, cloaked in symbolism to evade the censoring function of the conscious mind. His famous work, "The Interpretation of Dreams," published in 1899, delineated this theory and emphasized the concept of wish-fulfillment as the primary driver of dream content.

Freud's model classified dream elements into manifest and latent content. Manifest content refers to the actual images, thoughts, and feelings experienced in the dream, what one would narrate upon waking. Latent content, on the other hand, represents the unconscious wishes or desires that are the real motive forces behind the dream. In Freudian dream analysis, understanding the dream requires 'decoding' these symbols to unveil the latent content. Despite its groundbreaking nature, Freud's theories have been criticized for an over-emphasis on sexual and aggressive drives, and they do not account for all types of dreams, such as those that don't appear to contain repressed wishes.

Carl Jung and the Archetypal Approach

While Freud's student and later a peer, Carl Jung, also acknowledged the role of the unconscious in dreaming, his theories diverged significantly in focus and scope. Jung posited that dreams are not just outlets for individual unconscious desires but are also influenced by a deeper, collective unconscious shared across humanity. This collective unconscious, according to Jung, contains archetypes—universal symbols or themes that recur throughout human history and culture. Examples include motifs like the Hero, the Mother, and the Wise Old Man. These archetypes may appear in individual dreams but have collective meanings rooted in shared human experiences.

Jung also introduced the concept of individuation, a lifelong psychological process aimed at integrating different facets of the self into a coherent whole. He believed that dreams serve as guideposts or markers along this path to individuation. Instead of merely fulfilling repressed wishes, dreams, in Jung's view, could offer critical insights into one's emotional state, conflicts, and even potential for growth. Analyzing dreams from a Jungian perspective, therefore, involves not just decoding symbols but understanding their archetypal roots and their relevance to one's personal journey towards individuation.

Contemporary Developments

While Freud and Jung laid the foundations, modern psychology has expanded and diversified dream theories. Cognitive psychologists, for example, suggest that dreams may be a by-product of neural activity and the brain's way of processing information, devoid of deeper meaning. Another contemporary perspective is the threat simulation theory, which proposes that dreaming evolved as a form of cognitive rehearsal to prepare individuals for threats and challenges in waking life. Moreover, neuroscientific studies have started to investigate the neural substrates of dreaming, although a cohesive neuroscience-based theory of dreams remains elusive.

Summary

Dreams have been an object of fascination and inquiry throughout history. Psychological theories, initially propelled by Freud's psychoanalytic model and later diversified by Jung's archetypal framework, offer profound insights into why we dream and what these inner experiences signify. Although neither fully exhaustive nor universally accepted, these theories have set the stage for a richer understanding of the complex tapestry of human dreams. By integrating these theories into the broader context of spiritual and mystical practices, one can begin to appreciate dreams as multidimensional phenomena that engage not just the mind, but the deeper recesses of human experience and potential for growth.

CHAPTER 5: TYPES OF DREAMS AND THEIR MEANING

Dreams, those fleeting images and sensations that fill our nights, are more than just random play of the subconscious mind. They are a language, and like any language, they have dialects, genres, and styles. In other words, not all dreams are created equal. This chapter aims to explore various types of dreams that people commonly experience, including nightmares, lucid dreams, prophetic dreams, and more. Understanding these categories can deepen your insight into what your dreams are trying to communicate.

Nightmares and Their Symbolic Meanings

Nightmares, the dreams that evoke fear, anxiety, or sorrow, are common across all age groups. They often occur in times of stress, emotional turmoil, or when facing uncertainties. While they can be disturbing, their value should not be undermined. Nightmares are a form of emotional release and a signal that there is a situation or issue that you need to confront.

The symbolic meaning in nightmares often leans towards shadow aspects of oneself or one's life. For example, being chased in a dream often symbolizes running away from a problem or situation that you need to face. Natural disasters like tsunamis or earthquakes may represent overwhelming emotions or dramatic changes, respectively. Animals appearing in nightmares can be interpreted as repressed aspects of oneself; a ferocious dog could represent unacknowledged anger, for instance. Nightmares can serve as critical messages from the subconscious and may warrant a closer examination of your waking life.

Lucid Dreams: The Bridge to Conscious Dreaming

Lucid dreams are an intriguing category where the dreamer becomes aware that they are dreaming. This awareness allows for the possibility to control the events, settings, or characters within the dream. Lucid dreaming has been practiced for spiritual and psychological growth and is a cornerstone in Tibetan Dream Yoga and other mystical traditions.

The potential benefits of lucid dreaming are multifold. On a basic level, it offers a safe environment to practice and simulate real-life scenarios. More importantly, in spiritual practice, lucid dreaming can be a tool for shadow work, inner-child healing, and even dialoguing with higher aspects of consciousness. The dream landscape becomes a canvas on which you can project and resolve your deepest questions and fears. For many spiritual practitioners, lucid dreaming offers an accelerated path to self-awareness and transformation.

Prophetic Dreams and Synchronicities

Some dreams seem to go beyond the personal subconscious to tap into collective consciousness or even predict future events. Termed as prophetic or precognitive dreams, these are instances where the dream or elements within it correspond with future real-world events in an uncanny manner. It's a controversial area of study, both scientifically and spiritually, and opinions diverge on whether these dreams tap into a greater cosmic plan or are just coincidences.

In a mystical or spiritual framework, prophetic dreams could be interpreted as messages from the Divine or Universal Consciousness. They often carry a sense of urgency or importance that sets them apart from regular dreams. Synchronicities—meaningful coincidences—may follow such dreams, reinforcing their significance. For example, you might dream of meeting an old friend and then unexpectedly run into them the following week. While not all prophetic dreams have grand implications, they often serve as guideposts or validations of one's spiritual journey.

Summary

Types of dreams serve as the genre of the narrative your subconscious is trying to convey. Nightmares often symbolize shadow aspects and serve as a call to action. Lucid dreams offer an arena for personal and spiritual development, allowing an individual to engage with the subconscious actively. Prophetic dreams, though controversial, serve as guideposts or markers of synchronicity in one's life journey. Recognizing and understanding these categories not only adds another layer of interpretation but also provides targeted ways to integrate dreamwork into your broader spiritual practices.

CHAPTER 6: DECODING DREAM SYMBOLS

Dreams are rich tapestries woven from the threads of our subconscious mind, and to interpret them is to unravel layers of meaning buried within our psyche. Each dream element—be it an object, person, or scenario—serves as a symbol imbued with potential meanings. However, dream symbols are rarely straightforward; they often emerge from complex cultural, personal, and archetypal matrices. This chapter aims to serve as a primer on how to decode the most frequent symbols that appear in dreams, offering a nuanced approach that considers both universal archetypes and individual contexts.

Archetypal and Personal Symbols

The first step in decoding dream symbols is to differentiate between archetypal and personal symbols. Archetypal symbols are those that have universal meanings shared across various cultures and time periods. These symbols often relate to fundamental human experiences like birth, death, and love. Think of water, for instance, which commonly represents the emotional realm or the unconscious mind. In contrast, personal symbols are subjective; their meanings are unique to the dreamer and are influenced by individual experiences, relationships, and emotions. For example, a childhood home in a dream could symbolize comfort and security for one person but evoke memories of strife and tension for another.

Understanding the balance between archetypal and personal symbolism in dreams is vital for accurate interpretation. Archetypal symbols often serve as a foundational framework, but the subtleties and nuances that make a dream uniquely yours are usually captured by personal symbols. To decode these effectively, introspection and self-awareness are key. A dream journal can be invaluable in tracking recurring symbols and themes, helping you make connections between your dream world and waking life.

Common Dream Symbols and Interpretations

While the interpretation of dream symbols is subjective, certain symbols tend to recur in the dreams of many individuals and have been studied for their potential universal meanings. These include:

- **Water**: As mentioned earlier, water often symbolizes emotions or the unconscious mind. The condition of the water (clear, muddy, turbulent, calm) can offer additional layers of interpretation.
- **Animals**: Animals in dreams may symbolize primal instincts, desires, or fears. For instance, a lion might signify courage or represent an authoritative figure in your life.
- **Flying**: This is often linked to a desire for freedom or escape, but can also imply overconfidence or overlooking details.
- **Falling**: Generally associated with fears, insecurities, or perceived failings. It can also indicate feeling out of

control in some aspect of your life.

- **Houses or Buildings**: These usually represent the self or the mind. Different rooms can symbolize different facets of your personality or life experiences.
- **Roads**: Depending on their condition and direction, roads can symbolize your life's path, decisions, or a journey you are on or considering.

Being mindful of the context in which these symbols appear and your emotional response to them is crucial for a comprehensive understanding. For example, the symbol of water in a dream where you are drowning may have a very different meaning from a dream where you're peacefully sailing. The emotional tenor of the dream often provides clues to the symbol's significance.

The Fluidity of Dream Symbols

The interpretation of dream symbols is not a rigid or static process. Even universal symbols can alter their meanings based on the dream's context, your emotional state, or current life circumstances. Moreover, a symbol's meaning can evolve over time, reflecting your personal growth or changing situations. This fluidity underscores the importance of an ongoing, reflective practice of dream interpretation, rather than a one-time decoding. Revisiting older dreams in light of new life experiences can sometimes yield fresh insights.

In summary, decoding dream symbols is a nuanced endeavor that requires a balanced consideration of universal archetypes and personal experiences. Keeping track of recurring symbols and themes in a dream journal can provide invaluable insights into your subconscious mind. And remember, the meanings of symbols are not fixed; they are dynamic reflections of your evolving inner world. Therefore, the practice of dream interpretation is not just a key to understanding your subconscious, but also a door to ongoing personal growth and self-discovery.

CHAPTER 7: DREAM JOURNALS: YOUR PERSONAL ORACLE

Introduction

Dreams are a fascinating realm of unconscious processes, reflections of our daily lives, and possibly even mystical insights. However, the ephemeral nature of dreams can make it challenging to remember and interpret them fully. This chapter focuses on the essential tool for anyone serious about exploring the mystical aspects of their dreams: the dream journal. Keeping a dream journal can be an enlightening practice, serving as your personal oracle. It allows you to record, reflect on, and analyze your dreams, providing a crucial foundation for deeper dreamwork.

The Importance of a Dream Journal

Dreams are notoriously slippery. One moment you may be vividly experiencing a complex series of events in a dream, and the next moment, as you wake up, the details start to fade. It's as if your mind is a sieve, and the dream is like water trickling away. Many ancient and modern dream theorists, from Artemidorus of the Greco-Roman era to Carl Jung, have emphasized the importance of recording dreams as soon after waking as possible. The fading of dreams isn't merely an issue of memory; it also represents the loss of potential insights into your unconscious mind, emotional state, and even spiritual messages that might be encoded in the dream symbols.

A dream journal serves as a bridge between your unconscious and conscious realms, facilitating the interaction between the two. Recording your dreams diligently can make it easier to recognize patterns, recurring themes, or symbols that may be significant. By examining these elements, you can begin to decode the messages that your unconscious—or perhaps even a higher consciousness—is trying to communicate.

Effective Methods for Keeping a Dream Journal

Starting and maintaining a dream journal requires commitment but doesn't have to be a laborious task. Here are some methods to make the practice efficient and enriching:

Choose the Right Medium

First, decide what medium you're most comfortable using for your dream journal. This could be a physical notebook, a digital app, or even audio recordings. Each has its benefits and drawbacks. A physical notebook offers tangibility, but some may find typing or dictating dreams more efficient, especially given the semi-awake state in which you might find yourself recording them.

Immediate Recording

It is crucial to jot down your dreams as soon as you wake up. Even a delay of a few minutes can result in losing valuable details. Keep your journal or recording device within arm's reach of your bed to make this process as easy as possible.

Stream of Consciousness

Initially, don't worry about making sense of what you're writing. Your aim is to capture as much as you can remember. Write in a stream of consciousness manner, disregarding grammar and coherence. You can always go back to organize your thoughts later.

Include Specifics

Be as detailed as possible, including not just events but also the feelings, thoughts, and even smells or sounds that you can recall from the dream. The more comprehensive your notes, the richer the material you'll have for later analysis.

Date and Context

Always date your dream entries and include any life context that may be relevant. For example, note if you were under unusual stress, took any medications, or if significant life events occurred around the time of the dream. This context can be invaluable when you analyze the dream later.

Advanced Techniques for Utilizing a Dream Journal

Once you have a decent amount of entries, your dream journal can serve as a rich database for advanced dreamwork techniques. By consistently reviewing your journal, you can identify recurring symbols, settings, or characters. Such recurrent elements often hold particular significance, serving as keys to understanding deeper layers of your unconscious or even tapping into collective archetypes. Moreover, your dream journal can act as an insightful supplement to other spiritual practices or psychological therapies you may be engaged in, offering nuances that you might not capture through introspection alone.

Some dreamworkers also incorporate sketches or diagrams to capture non-verbal elements of dreams. This multimedia approach can provide an even richer palette for analysis and interpretation, enabling a fuller integration of dream insights into your waking life. Additionally, your dream journal can be an excellent resource for any form of dream sharing or collective dream interpretation practices you may participate in, offering you a structured and detailed account to draw upon.

Summary

A dream journal isn't merely a diary but a potent tool for personal growth, spiritual exploration, and psychological insight. By consistently recording your dreams, you're not only preserving the raw data for future interpretation but also facilitating a deeper dialogue between your conscious and unconscious selves. The journal becomes your personal oracle, a sacred text that can help unravel the complexities of your inner world. Thus, for anyone committed to the exploration of dreams, keeping a dream journal is not an optional exercise but an essential practice.

CHAPTER 8: DREAMING AND THE CHAKRA SYSTEM

Introduction

Dreaming and the chakra system have both been topics of spiritual and philosophical inquiry for centuries. While dreaming serves as a gateway to the unconscious mind, the chakra system functions as a metaphysical anatomy of spiritual centers within the body. These two seemingly disparate subjects can be analyzed in unison to offer a holistic view of both psychological and spiritual health. In this chapter, we will delve into the intricate relationship between dreams and the chakras to understand how they interact, influence each other, and can be integrated into a unified practice of spiritual growth and self-understanding.

The Chakra System: A Brief Overview

Before diving into the relationship between dreams and the chakra system, it's essential to grasp the basics of what chakras are. Originating from ancient Indian spiritual traditions, the word 'chakra' translates to 'wheel' or 'disk' in Sanskrit. In the context of spiritual anatomy, chakras are energy centers that align along the spine, starting at the base and ending at the crown of the head. Each chakra corresponds to specific physiological and psychological functions, as well as different states of consciousness.

Traditionally, there are seven major chakras:

1. **Root Chakra (Muladhara)**: Located at the base of the spine, it governs survival, security, and basic human needs.
2. **Sacral Chakra (Svadhishthana)**: Situated in the lower abdomen, it controls pleasure, creativity, and emotional balance.
3. **Solar Plexus Chakra (Manipura)**: Found in the upper abdomen, it manages self-esteem, personal power, and individual will.
4. **Heart Chakra (Anahata)**: Located at the heart center, it is tied to love, compassion, and acceptance.
5. **Throat Chakra (Vishuddha)**: Situated in the throat, it governs communication and expression.
6. **Third Eye Chakra (Ajna)**: Found in the forehead, between the eyes, it controls intuition, imagination, and insight.
7. **Crown Chakra (Sahasrara)**: Located at the top of the head, it governs spiritual connection and enlightenment.

Each chakra has its own set of characteristics, including a designated color, sound frequency, and associated bodily organs. An imbalance in any of these chakras is thought to manifest as physical or emotional ailments, affecting both well-being and spiritual progress.

Interplay Between Dreams and Chakras

As dream narratives often arise from the subconscious mind,

they can serve as windows into our inner world, including the state of our chakras. The symbols, emotions, and scenarios presented in dreams may point toward imbalances or activations in specific chakras. For instance, dreams centered around survival, home, or family could be associated with the Root Chakra. Likewise, dreams featuring communication struggles might be connected to an imbalance in the Throat Chakra.

Moreover, some spiritual practitioners claim to experience vivid dreams that directly correspond to the opening or balancing of certain chakras. These dreams may contain symbolic elements like colors or animals that are traditionally associated with the respective chakra. For example, dreaming of a serpent rising along the spine could signify the awakening of the Kundalini energy, a primal force believed to reside at the base of the spine, related to the Root Chakra.

Just as dreams can give insight into the chakra system, mindfulness of the chakras can also enrich your dream experience. For example, focusing on the Third Eye Chakra during meditation before sleep can heighten your intuitive and insightful aspects of dreaming, possibly leading to more frequent lucid dreams.

Integrating Chakras into Dreamwork

Understanding the connection between dreams and chakras can lead to a more nuanced approach to dream interpretation and spiritual practice. Here are some ways to integrate the two:

- **Dream Journaling with a Chakra Focus**: When jotting down dreams, note any themes or symbols that could be associated with particular chakras. This focus will deepen your interpretation and provide actionable insights for balancing your chakras.

- **Chakra-based Meditation before Sleep**: Engage in chakra meditations before sleep to activate or balance certain chakras, with the intent of influencing the type or quality of your dreams.
- **Mindful Interpretation**: When interpreting your dreams, consider them within the framework of your current chakra states. Are you undergoing a period of emotional upheaval? Your dreams and the state of your Sacral or Heart Chakra could be interconnected.

Incorporating chakra awareness into your dreamwork can result in a synergistic practice that addresses not just your subconscious mind but your spiritual anatomy as well. It can contribute to a more holistic approach to self-understanding and spiritual growth.

Conclusion

The realms of dreams and the chakra system are vast and rich with symbolic language. Each offers a unique lens to view the self, yet together, they provide a holistic approach to understanding our complex psychological and spiritual makeup. The interconnectedness of these systems invites us to explore deeper levels of consciousness, offering a nuanced route to personal growth and enlightenment. By paying attention to the subtle cues and symbols in our dreams related to chakras, we can foster a more harmonious balance within our spiritual anatomy, thereby enriching our overall well-being and spiritual journey.

CHAPTER 9: CULTURAL CONTEXTS OF DREAM INTERPRETATION

Introduction

In exploring the multi-faceted world of dreams, it's crucial to recognize that interpretations are not monolithic. While universal themes may emerge, the lens through which we view these dream symbols can vary dramatically from culture to culture. Understanding these cultural nuances not only enriches our comprehension of dream symbols but also provides a more holistic perspective on how dreams fit into the broader tapestry of human experience. This chapter delves into the role of cultural contexts in dream interpretation, highlighting key traditions and practices that showcase the diversity of perspectives in this fascinating field.

Indigenous Dreaming Traditions

Indigenous cultures around the world have rich, complex relationships with the realm of dreams. For many of these cultures, dreams serve as more than just random occurrences during sleep; they are profound experiences that connect individuals to ancestral wisdom, spiritual realms, and even predictive insights.

For example, among the Aboriginal peoples of Australia, the Dreamtime is a foundational concept that speaks to the creation of the world and the beings within it. Dreams serve as a bridge to this primordial era, offering glimpses into the spiritual and the metaphysical. The Dreamtime is not confined to the past; it is a living energy that continues to shape the present and the future.

In Native American cultures, dreams often serve as visions that can guide individuals or entire communities. Specific animals appearing in dreams, such as the eagle or the wolf, are seen as totems and messengers, offering guidance and wisdom. Some tribes also have designated "dream interpreters," who are skilled in deciphering the symbols and themes that manifest during dream states.

Eastern Philosophies and Dreams

Eastern philosophies like Hinduism, Buddhism, and Daoism also offer unique perspectives on dream interpretation. In Hindu tradition, dreams are considered to be one of the sixteen "kalas," or phases of the moon, related to stages of human consciousness. Hindu scriptures speak about dream states as a separate reality that offers clues about past and future lives. Some traditional interpretations even categorize dreams into three types: those influenced by divine figures, those reflecting the dreamer's state of mind, and those that are simply chaotic.

Buddhist dream interpretation, often linked with Tibetan Dream Yoga practices, perceives dreams as illusions. The goal is not necessarily to interpret these dreams but to realize their illusory nature, a realization that can help awaken the dreamer to greater spiritual awareness in both the dreaming and waking states.

In Daoism, dreams are viewed as interplays of yin and yang

energies. According to Daoist beliefs, dreams can offer insights into the balance or imbalance of these fundamental energies in an individual's life, and therefore can serve as tools for personal and spiritual development.

Western Psychological Models

Western traditions, influenced predominantly by the works of Sigmund Freud and Carl Jung, have largely taken a psychological approach to dream interpretation. Freud's psychoanalytic theory considered dreams as the "royal road to the unconscious," where repressed desires and conflicts could surface. Jung introduced the concept of archetypes—universal symbols found across different cultures but also subject to cultural variations in their interpretation. For instance, water might universally signify emotion but could have different connotations depending on cultural mores and myths.

Summary

Culture plays a significant role in shaping how we understand and interpret dreams. From indigenous traditions that connect dreams to ancestral and spiritual wisdom, to Eastern philosophies that integrate dreams into broader spiritual practices, to Western psychological models that seek to unearth the unconscious mind, the landscape of dream interpretation is incredibly varied. These diverse perspectives enrich our understanding and offer various pathways to explore the rich tapestry of the dream world. The key takeaway is that while dreams may speak a universal language of symbols, those symbols are read through the unique dictionaries of our diverse cultures. By considering these cultural contexts, we add depth and nuance to our quest for understanding the mystical and intriguing world of dreams.

CHAPTER 10: THE SCIENTIFIC PERSPECTIVE ON DREAMS

Dreams have been a subject of human curiosity for centuries, with various cultures and spiritual traditions offering their own interpretations and understandings. While earlier chapters in this book explored the mystical, psychological, and cultural perspectives on dreams, this chapter will delve into the scientific standpoint. In particular, we will look at neurological findings, sleep cycle research, and experimental psychology that have contributed to our understanding of dreaming.

Neurobiology of Dreaming

Perhaps the most direct approach to understanding dreams scientifically is through neurobiology, which allows researchers to see which parts of the brain are active during different phases of sleep. Using tools like electroencephalograms (EEGs) and functional magnetic resonance imaging (fMRI), scientists have been able to determine that the majority of vivid dreaming occurs during Rapid Eye Movement (REM) sleep. During this phase, the brain is almost as active as when it is awake, leading to vivid and sometimes lucid dreams.

Interestingly, neurobiological studies have also highlighted the involvement of certain brain regions and neurotransmitters during dreaming. The limbic system, which is responsible for emotions and memory, is highly active. This might explain why dreams are often emotionally charged and sometimes draw upon memories or variants of them. The prefrontal cortex, responsible for logical reasoning and decision-making, is less active during dreams, which might account for the sometimes surreal and illogical nature of dream content.

Sleep Cycles and Dream Patterns

Understanding the sleep cycle provides another layer of insight into the scientific study of dreams. A full sleep cycle comprises four stages of non-REM sleep, followed by a REM stage, usually lasting around 90 minutes in total for adults. As the night progresses, REM stages lengthen, leading to longer and more vivid dreams toward the early morning hours. Research has shown that disruption in sleep cycles can affect dreaming patterns and even lead to sleep disorders that influence the content and emotional tone of dreams.

Dreaming isn't confined solely to REM sleep, although those dreams tend to be the most vivid and memorable. Studies indicate that we also experience dreams during non-REM stages, although these dreams are often less vivid and may not be as emotionally charged. Some theories propose that non-REM dreams serve different cognitive functions than REM dreams, though this is still a subject of ongoing research.

Experimental Psychology and Dream Research

Experimental psychology has offered yet another angle through which to view dreaming, primarily focusing on the cognitive aspects. One area of study aims to understand dream function, positing theories ranging from emotional regulation to problem-solving. For example, the 'threat simulation theory' suggests that dreaming serves as a kind of cognitive rehearsal for real-life challenges, enabling the brain to practice responses to potential threats.

Another interesting area of research is the study of dream recall. Not all dreams are remembered upon waking, and experimental psychology has aimed to understand what factors contribute to dream recall. Factors like emotional intensity, proximity to waking, and individual differences in cognitive style can all impact whether a dream is remembered or forgotten.

The integration of scientific perspectives with other modes of understanding dreams can offer a comprehensive view. For instance, the neuroscience of dreaming can potentially explain why certain kinds of meditation or visualization exercises appear to influence dream content. By the same token, understanding sleep cycles can be immensely useful in dream incubation techniques aimed at invoking specific kinds of dreams. Even cognitive theories, like the threat simulation model, have intriguing overlaps with spiritual interpretations that see dreams as precognitive or offering guidance for life challenges.

In summary, the scientific perspective on dreams serves as a valuable complement to spiritual and mystical interpretations. It grounds dream phenomena in empirical observations and offers avenues for interdisciplinary research. While the scientific lens may not capture the entirety of human experience surrounding dreams, it provides foundational knowledge that helps demystify some aspects of this fascinating mental activity.

CHAPTER 11: DREAM IMAGERY AND ARCHETYPES

Introduction

In the realm of dream interpretation, one cannot overlook the role of imagery and archetypes. These universal symbols are deeply embedded in the collective unconscious and serve as a common thread weaving through individual dream experiences. This chapter delves into the origin, nature, and significance of dream imagery and archetypes, exploring how they interact with personal and collective layers of the subconscious mind.

The Origin of Archetypes

The concept of archetypes originates from the work of Swiss psychologist Carl Jung. Jung postulated that archetypes are primordial images or patterns that are part of the collective unconscious, shared across cultures and generations. These are not learned or acquired through experience; rather, they exist as a form of inherited mental content. Archetypes manifest through various mediums such as myths, legends, and, notably, dreams. They emerge as universal symbols like the Mother, the Hero, the Sage, and so forth, appearing in individual dreams but reflecting collective, shared meanings.

The concept has roots in Platonic philosophy, which posits that all things have an essential form, an ideal that exists independent of individual instances. In the same way, archetypal images in dreams are seen as the ideal forms of particular concepts or experiences. They serve as the foundational blueprints that guide the structures and themes of our dreams. Because archetypes are universal, their manifestations can be found in folklore, religious texts, and art, extending far beyond individual or cultural experiences.

The Role of Dream Imagery

While archetypes serve as the universal framework, dream imagery fills in the details. Think of archetypes as the skeletal structure of a building and dream imagery as the bricks, windows, and decorative elements that complete it. Dream imagery is often deeply personal and influenced by an individual's experiences, beliefs, and emotional state. It includes specific settings, characters, and objects that populate a dream, offering nuance to the broader archetypal themes.

For example, if the archetype of the "Hero's Journey" is manifested in a dream, the specific imagery might include a labyrinth, a monster, or a treasure, which are personalized details meaningful to the dreamer. These images may be shaped by recent experiences, unresolved emotional issues, or unique aspirations. Therefore, dream imagery acts as an interface between the universal and the personal, linking archetypal patterns with individual life circumstances.

Interpreting Archetypes and Imagery

The interpretation of dream archetypes and imagery can be a deeply insightful process. It's a way of translating the language of the subconscious into comprehensible terms. Often, this involves considering both the collective and personal aspects of a dream. The collective aspect draws from shared human experiences and cultural contexts that inform the archetypal themes. The personal aspect involves the specific circumstances and emotions of the individual dreamer.

To successfully interpret a dream, one must operate at the intersection of these dimensions. For instance, a serpent appearing in a dream could symbolize transformation or danger at the archetypal level, as these are common cultural and mythological connotations. However, the personal significance may vary for the dreamer based on their experiences, such as a fear of snakes or recent changes in life. Thus, recognizing an archetype provides the general framework for understanding a dream, while the particular imagery offers clues to its specific relevance for the dreamer.

The process is both intuitive and analytical, requiring an open mind that can navigate the abstract terrain of the subconscious. This process also benefits from a multi-disciplinary approach, incorporating insights from psychology, mythology, religion, and even literature, to enrich the understanding of dream symbols.

Summary

Dream imagery and archetypes are intertwined elements that provide the vocabulary and grammar of our dreaming mind. Archetypes offer universal themes and structures that resonate across humanity, serving as the essential forms of various concepts or experiences. Dream imagery, on the other hand, is the personalized manifestation of these themes, nuanced by individual circumstances and emotions. Together, they create a complex, rich tapestry that we can decipher to gain profound insights into our subconscious mind and, by extension, our waking life.

CHAPTER 12: ANIMAL TOTEMS AND DREAM SYMBOLISM

In the realm of dream symbolism, animals often appear as messengers bearing insights and wisdom from the subconscious or the spiritual world. Animals in dreams can serve as guides, guardians, or manifestations of qualities you need to pay attention to. As we delve into this beginner's guide to animal totems and dream symbolism, we will explore how these creatures contribute to the intricate tapestry of our dreaming minds. By becoming attuned to the roles animals play in our dreams, we can glean valuable insights into our own psyches as well as our broader spiritual paths.

The Basic Tenets of Animal Symbolism

Animal symbolism predates recorded history and exists in almost every culture and spiritual tradition. In ancient Egyptian cosmology, for instance, animals were often associated with gods and goddesses. In Native American spirituality, animals are considered spirit guides, each endowed with specific teachings and wisdom. In Hinduism, animals are also venerated, often as vehicles or avatars of gods.

The appearance of animals in your dreams often carries specific symbolic weight based on these age-old interpretations. For example, seeing a hawk might be an indicator of the need for focused vision and observation in your waking life. Similarly, dreaming of a snake could signify transformation or change, given its ability to shed its skin.

However, it's crucial to remember that the meaning of an animal appearing in a dream can also be highly personalized. Your personal experiences and feelings towards a specific animal can add a layer of complexity to its conventional symbolic meaning. Hence, interpreting animal symbols in dreams is a nuanced exercise that involves a mix of traditional understanding and individual introspection.

Cultural Variations and Personal Associations

The interpretation of animal symbolism in dreams is not a one-size-fits-all endeavor. Different cultures can have varying beliefs about the same animal, which can lead to different interpretations. For instance, in Western culture, an owl is generally considered a symbol of wisdom, but in some African traditions, it is associated with death or witchcraft.

Personal experience and sentiment also play a significant role in dream interpretation. If you had a traumatic experience with a dog in your childhood, dreaming about a dog might evoke fear or caution, even if dogs are generally seen as symbols of loyalty and companionship.

Integration into Dreamwork and Spiritual Practices

Identifying and understanding the role of animal totems in your dreams is not merely an academic exercise but can be a pivotal part of your spiritual journey. Recognizing these symbols and integrating them into your waking life can be empowering. Some people choose to incorporate the power or lesson of their dream animal into their spiritual rituals, meditations, or even their daily affirmations.

You can also consider keeping a separate section in your dream journal dedicated to animal encounters. This can help you track recurring patterns or themes and might offer you a nuanced understanding of your current spiritual or emotional state. Moreover, studying the animals that frequently appear can guide you to relevant literature, mythologies, and cultural practices that resonate with you, allowing you to deepen your spiritual understanding and personal growth.

Summary

Animal totems in dreams serve as powerful symbols with rich historical, cultural, and personal implications. They can appear as messengers offering wisdom, as guides leading you toward a particular path, or as reflections of specific qualities you need to focus on. While the understanding of these symbols often involves traditional wisdom, it is equally shaped by personal experiences and cultural nuances. Including the study of animal symbols into your dreamwork can provide invaluable insights and contribute significantly to your spiritual journey. Through earnest interpretation and integration, you can enhance not only your understanding of your dreams but also your broader spiritual practice.

CHAPTER 13: DREAM SYMBOLS IN LITERATURE AND MYTHOLOGY

Dreams have played a pivotal role in human imagination since time immemorial. They've been potent sources of storytelling, spiritual insight, and philosophical contemplation. This chapter aims to explore the intricate relationship between dream symbols and their representation in literature and mythology. We will delve into how literary works and myths not only capture the essence of dreams but also contribute to the lexicon of symbols that many people recognize in their own nocturnal visions.

Classical Literature and Dream Symbols

In classical literature, dreams often serve as omens or prophecy. For instance, in Homer's "The Iliad," a dream sent by Zeus delivers a message to Agamemnon, influencing his strategy in the Trojan War. Dreams in such contexts are usually not just random occurrences but are laden with cultural and narrative significance. They incorporate symbols that have specific implications within the framework of the story. A snake, an eagle, or an object like a sword in these dreams could embody courage, divine intervention, or impending conflict, and are generally reflective of the broader societal understanding of these symbols at the time.

The ancient Greek tragedies, like those by Aeschylus, Sophocles, and Euripides, often included dreams to foreshadow events or reveal psychological intricacies. In the tragedy "Oedipus Rex," Jocasta dismisses a prophecy that came to her husband, Laius, in a dream, only to realize the devastating truth later. In such literary contexts, dreams and their symbols become a plot device that underscores a tragic irony.

Dreams in Religious Texts and Mythology

Religious texts offer another rich reservoir of dream symbolism. In the Judeo-Christian tradition, Joseph's ability to interpret dreams saves Egypt from famine, as narrated in the Old Testament. His understanding of dream symbols like cows and grains, their numbers and conditions, exemplify how culturally embedded the act of dream interpretation can be. These symbols are deeply entrenched in the agrarian society of ancient Egypt and translate into practical wisdom through Joseph's interpretation.

Similarly, in Hindu mythology, dreams serve as powerful metaphors and teaching tools. For instance, in the epic Mahabharata, Yudhishthira dreams of a half-eaten mango, symbolizing the partial virtues he's acquired and signifying the ultimate impermanence of all things. These narratives employ dream symbolism as more than just an allegorical device; they provide moral and spiritual lessons.

In Native American myths, dreams often function as gateways to other dimensions or as means of communication with spiritual entities. Animals in these dreams are seen as totems that embody specific qualities or messages from the spiritual realm. A raven might symbolize transformation, while a bear could represent introspection and strength.

Modern Literature and the Interpretation of Dream Symbols

Modern literature has delved into the realm of the unconscious mind more explicitly. Authors like Franz Kafka and James Joyce employ dream logic and symbols to disturb and question the nature of reality and identity. Kafka's "The Metamorphosis," where the protagonist wakes up as a giant insect, utilizes the dream-like absurdity to probe issues of alienation and existential despair. James Joyce's "Finnegans Wake" is almost an extended dream sequence, densely populated with symbols borrowed from various cultural and mythological sources.

Contemporary works often extend beyond mere plot devices or allegories, exploring the psychological depths of the characters through their dreams. Symbols like water, mirrors, or labyrinths make frequent appearances in modern literature, mimicking the shared unconscious of humanity and offering a plethora of interpretations.

In summary, dream symbols in literature and mythology provide a fascinating avenue to understand both the collective imagination and individual psychology. They function not just as storytelling elements but as windows into the complexities of human thought, emotion, and spirituality. From ancient epics to modern narratives, the interplay of dreams and symbols adds layers of meaning, enriching our interpretive capabilities and inviting us to look within and beyond.

CHAPTER 14: ETHICS OF DREAM INTERPRETATION

Introduction

Dreams have fascinated humanity since time immemorial, serving as a playground for our subconscious and a tool for spiritual, emotional, and even physical introspection. While earlier chapters delved into the language, history, and mechanics of dreams, this chapter tackles a less frequently discussed but equally critical topic: the ethics of dream interpretation. The act of interpreting dreams is fraught with ethical considerations that many overlook. This chapter elucidates the ethical boundaries to be respected when dealing with personal or shared dream content, ensuring the practice is conducted responsibly and conscientiously.

Ethical Self-Interrogation

Before delving into the analysis of any dream—your own or someone else's—it is crucial to pause and self-interrogate. The questions to ask oneself are multifold: What is my motive behind analyzing this dream? Do I possess the necessary knowledge and sensitivity to explore its dimensions? Am I prepared to confront potentially uncomfortable truths?

The realm of dreams often blurs the line between conscious and unconscious aspects of our psyches, revealing vulnerabilities or facets of our nature that we might not be fully cognizant of. Incorrect or misguided interpretation can lead to undue stress, psychological discomfort, or even a spiraling sense of confusion. This risk is particularly acute when a dream's subject matter pertains to emotional trauma or deeply rooted insecurities. Consequently, maintaining ethical vigilance is indispensable for responsible dream interpretation.

Ethical Guidelines for Interpreting Others' Dreams

When it comes to interpreting other people's dreams, the ethical landscape becomes even more complicated. Here are some key considerations:

Informed Consent

Before diving into someone else's subconscious world, it is ethically crucial to obtain their explicit consent. This might seem obvious, but dream sharing often occurs spontaneously, in casual conversations. Even if the dreamer initiates the topic, it is good practice to ask if they are comfortable with you offering an interpretation.

Confidentiality

Dreams can reveal intensely personal, potentially embarrassing, or sensitive information. When someone trusts you with their dream, that trust should be honored. Unless explicitly permitted, the information shared should remain confidential.

Expertise and Scope

Unless you are a certified therapist, psychologist, or a recognized expert in dream interpretation, it's important to refrain from giving medical or professional advice based on dream content. Even within professional circles, ethical considerations necessitate avoiding overreach or unsubstantiated conclusions.

Emotional Sensitivity

Dreams can serve as outlets for our most profound fears, hopes, and vulnerabilities. Consequently, they should be handled with the utmost emotional sensitivity. Brusque or insensitive interpretations can leave a dreamer feeling exposed or judged. Therefore, fostering an atmosphere of emotional safety and openness is vital.

Avoiding Presumptiveness

Each individual's dream landscape is intricately personalized, steeped in their unique experiences, fears, and desires. Even widely accepted archetypes can manifest differently depending on individual psychology and life experiences. It's ethically irresponsible to jump to conclusions or force-fit interpretations.

Summary

Dream interpretation, while a captivating and enlightening pursuit, comes with a responsibility that extends beyond mere curiosity or intrigue. It delves into the intimate recesses of the human psyche and thus mandates an ethical approach. Whether you're exploring your dreams or helping others understand theirs, ethical vigilance is not just an optional extra but a necessary cornerstone. Balancing the thirst for understanding with ethical considerations ensures that the journey into the dream realm is both enlightening and respectful.

CHAPTER 15: A PRACTICAL GUIDE TO BEGINNER DREAMWORK

Dreamwork is a broad and versatile field that lends itself to both intellectual scrutiny and mystical exploration. As we've traversed the initial chapters covering the basics of dream theory, symbols, ethics, and cultural contexts, we're now entering a phase where action steps are vital. This chapter aims to offer a step-by-step guide for those who are new to dreamwork but are keen to dive in. We'll cover setting intentions, recording dreams, and a handful of analysis techniques that can set the stage for deeper exploration in subsequent chapters.

Setting the Stage: The Importance of Intentions

In dreamwork, as in any spiritual or psychological endeavor, intention-setting is paramount. Setting a clear intention before you sleep can prime your subconscious mind to present you with dreams that are aligned with your areas of focus. It doesn't have to be complicated; a simple sentence will suffice. For instance, if you wish to gain insight into a relationship, you might set an intention like, "I am open to receiving wisdom about my relationship with [Name]." Or perhaps you're concerned about a decision you have to make. In this case, an intention might be, "I welcome guidance about [Decision] in my dreams tonight."

What's fascinating about intention-setting is that it acts like a compass for your subconscious. By signaling what you're focusing on, you are more likely to have dreams that resonate with that particular subject or theme. It's akin to setting a destination in your internal GPS, leading to a journey filled with pertinent landmarks and signs.

Keeping a Dream Journal: The Subconscious Unveiled

We touched briefly on the importance of keeping a dream journal in Chapter 7, but let's go into the practicalities here. A dream journal can be a simple notebook, a digital document, or even a dedicated app—choose whatever feels most accessible and comfortable for you. Place it within arm's reach of your bed, along with a pen or other writing utensil. The key is to jot down your dreams immediately upon waking, as they can dissipate quickly from conscious memory.

When recording your dream, focus on the following elements:

- **Characters**: Who appeared in your dream? Were they people you know or strangers? Were there animals?
- **Setting**: Where did the dream take place? Was it a real or imagined location?
- **Actions and Events**: What happened in the dream? Was there a discernible sequence of events or plot?
- **Emotional Tone**: How did you feel during the dream? Was there a shift in emotions at any point?
- **Symbols and Oddities**: Were there any recurring symbols, strange objects, or peculiar happenings?

The purpose of this meticulous documentation is to provide a rich landscape that you can later analyze, compare, and interpret.

Beginner Techniques for Dream Analysis

Once you've collected a few dream entries, you can start to perform some basic analysis. Here are some foundational techniques:

1. **Symbol Clustering**: Review your dream journal and note any recurring symbols or themes. Group them together and look for patterns. For instance, if you frequently dream of water, consider the context in which it appears—calm lakes might signify emotional tranquility, whereas turbulent oceans could indicate chaos.

2. **Dialogue Technique**: This method involves having an imagined conversation with an element or character from your dream. Sit quietly, visualize the character or object, and ask it questions like, "Why are you appearing in my dream?" or "What message do you have for me?" You may be surprised by the intuitive insights that arise.

3. **Reality Checks**: These are techniques borrowed from lucid dreaming practices but can be useful for anyone delving into dreamwork. Periodically throughout your waking day, ask yourself, "Am I dreaming?" This practice not only increases your likelihood of having a lucid dream but also strengthens your ability to remember your dreams.

Armed with these foundational steps and techniques, you'll be better prepared to explore the labyrinthine corridors of your subconscious mind. You've learned to set intentions to guide your dream content, keep a dream journal to record what unfolds, and apply some basic methods to start making sense of your dreams. These are your initial tools in the toolkit of dreamwork, equipping you for the more complex topics and techniques that await in later chapters. With this groundwork laid, you're ready to delve deeper into the mystical and transformative realm of dreams.

CHAPTER 16: ADVANCED DREAM JOURNALING TECHNIQUES

Introduction

As you journey deeper into the realm of dream exploration, the tools you use must evolve to capture the nuances and intricate layers of your nocturnal experiences. While the initial chapters introduced you to the concept of keeping a dream journal, this chapter aims to deepen your understanding of advanced journaling techniques. These methods will help you glean greater insight from your dreams, enriching your spiritual practices and personal growth.

Dynamic Categorization

One of the shortcomings of basic journaling is its linear and narrative-focused structure, which may not fully capture the multidimensional essence of dreams. An advanced approach involves dynamic categorization, where you classify different elements of your dreams into categories or themes.

For instance, you could identify recurring motifs, like "water," "flight," or "animals." By doing so, you'll soon recognize patterns, such as how water often symbolizes emotional states, or animals as totems or archetypes.

Beyond this, some people adopt a more elaborate classification scheme that integrates colors, numbers, or even astrological signs corresponding to the dream's date. The primary benefit of this system is its capacity to reveal subtler connections between dreams over time, which might remain hidden in a straightforward narrative format.

Layered Analysis

Another advanced technique is layered analysis. At first glance, dreams may appear as jumbled sequences with disjointed elements. However, upon closer examination, you may identify multiple layers of symbolism, metaphors, and hidden meanings.

Here, layered analysis involves a multi-pronged approach. First, conduct an initial narrative recounting, as you would in a basic journal. This serves as your baseline understanding of the dream. Next, delve deeper to identify archetypal symbols, personal references, or mystical aspects. For instance, a simple scene where you find yourself in a forest might initially symbolize "adventure" or "uncertainty." But if you observe an owl in the same dream, a layered analysis might reveal the coexistence of wisdom (the owl) within uncertainty (the forest).

Another layer could be an emotional or kinesthetic analysis. How did the dream make you feel? Did you experience bodily sensations? What are the implications of these experiences on your waking life? With practice, layered analysis can provide a holistic understanding of your dreamscape, something rudimentary journaling may miss.

Integration with Other Spiritual Practices

By now, you may have experimented with various spiritual practices like meditation, chakra work, or tarot readings. Advanced dream journaling is not an isolated exercise but can be effectively integrated into these practices.

For instance, you might meditate on a dream symbol and record any insights that surface. Alternatively, after a tarot reading, you could cross-reference any symbolic parallels in your recent dreams. This complementary approach enriches both your dreamwork and other spiritual activities, making the journal a nexus for your multidimensional spiritual journey.

Mindfulness and Recall Enhancement

The benefits of advanced dream journaling are augmented when coupled with mindfulness techniques. Through focused breathing and setting intentions before sleep, you can improve dream recall. Advanced practitioners also use techniques like "anchoring," where a particular stimulus (like a scent or a piece of music) is associated with the practice of journaling. Over time, this stimulus aids in more lucid dream states and easier recall, facilitating a more effective journaling process.

Summary

Advanced dream journaling goes beyond the simple act of recounting experiences. By adopting techniques like dynamic categorization, layered analysis, and integration with other spiritual practices, you enrich your understanding of your dreamscape, allowing for more profound insights and personal growth. In addition, mindful approaches can enhance recall and lucidity, making the journaling process itself a more intricate tapestry of your spiritual journey. As you evolve in your dreamwork, your journal becomes less of a passive repository and more of an active tool for introspection and transformation.

CHAPTER 17: DREAMS AND ALTERED STATES OF CONSCIOUSNESS

Introduction

As we transition from beginner-level content into the intermediate realm of dream studies, Chapter 17 delves into the intriguing relationship between dreams and altered states of consciousness. Altered states are variations of mental conditions that diverge significantly from ordinary waking states. Meditation, trance, hypnosis, and even certain drug-induced states fall under this category. Understanding the dynamics between altered states and dreams can offer valuable insights into the malleability of human consciousness and contribute to a holistic approach in dreamwork.

The Phenomenology of Altered States

Altered states of consciousness can manifest in various forms, ranging from the deep introspective experiences seen in meditation to the dissociative states invoked by hypnosis or specific substances. These states often involve shifts in perception, emotional regulation, cognitive function, and self-awareness. Research has shown that certain brainwave patterns, different from those in the regular waking state, are associated with altered states of consciousness.

It's important to draw parallels between these characteristics and the phenomenology of dreaming. Dreams, like altered states, offer a departure from ordinary experience and cognition. They can evoke deep emotional responses, transport us to surreal landscapes, and present paradoxical situations that challenge our conventional understanding of reality. Both dreams and altered states serve as windows into the subconscious, revealing facets of the mind that are often veiled in ordinary consciousness.

The Shared Architecture of Dream and Altered States

Dreams and altered states share structural similarities in the way the human brain functions during these periods. In both conditions, the prefrontal cortex, responsible for rational thinking and decision-making, exhibits reduced activity. Simultaneously, regions linked with emotional processing and memory retrieval become more active. This neural shift allows for a more fluid, associative mode of thinking that circumvents the critical, logical filters that usually dominate waking life.

Another striking similarity is the occurrence of archetypal symbols and narrative patterns. In both dreams and altered states induced by methods like shamanic drumming or deep meditation, individuals frequently report encountering symbols or entities that resonate with archetypal motifs. These could range from meeting a "wise old man" to confronting a "shadowy" figure. While the interpretation may differ based on individual and cultural contexts, the recurrence of such symbols suggests a shared archetypal reservoir that becomes accessible during these altered modes of consciousness.

Practical Applications in Dreamwork

Understanding the relationship between dreams and altered states can yield valuable techniques for dreamwork. For instance, specific meditative practices designed to induce altered states can be employed just before sleep to "program" the mind for lucid dreaming or problem-solving dreams. Conversely, insights obtained from dream experiences can be actively meditated upon in altered states to achieve greater emotional clarity or deeper spiritual insights.

In disciplines like shamanism or tantric practices, the seamless integration of dreamwork and altered states is foundational. These traditions often involve rituals designed to blur the lines between waking and dreaming consciousness, utilizing the complementary nature of these states to facilitate healing, divination, or spiritual awakening.

Summary

In this chapter, we have navigated the complex but enriching landscape of altered states of consciousness and their relationship with dreams. By examining their shared phenomenological and neurological underpinnings, we recognize that dreams and altered states serve as complementary avenues for exploring the intricacies of human consciousness. Moreover, the conscious blending of techniques derived from both can prove invaluable in advanced dreamwork, enabling a deeper and more nuanced understanding of the self and the metaphysical dimensions it can access.

CHAPTER 18: SYNCHRONICITIES: THE ROLE OF DREAMS IN DAILY LIFE

Introduction

As we venture deeper into the intricate tapestry of dreams and their interpretations, a mysterious yet fascinating aspect beckons for exploration—synchronicities. These are meaningful coincidences that blur the boundaries between the dreaming and waking states. Such synchronicities often appear as 'nudges,' guiding us toward personal or spiritual growth, if we choose to heed them. In this chapter, we will scrutinize the concept of synchronicity in dreams, examine its historical background, and delve into its spiritual and practical implications.

Historical Perspective: Jung's Synchronicity

Carl Jung, the Swiss psychiatrist and psychoanalyst, was one of the first modern thinkers to give serious attention to the phenomenon of synchronicity. Jung postulated that synchronicities were not mere random occurrences but constituted an "acausal connecting principle" that linked the inner world of the psyche with the outer world of reality. In Jung's view, the emergence of similar symbols or events in both waking life and dreams wasn't coincidental but indicative of deeper, underlying patterns and meanings.

Jung proposed that synchronicities served to connect the unconscious with the conscious mind, functioning as bridges between different states of awareness. His theory opened the door for integrating psychology with elements of spirituality, metaphysics, and even quantum mechanics. The quantum perspective considers the universe as fundamentally interconnected at the sub-atomic level, which could potentially provide a scientific basis for the phenomenon of synchronicity, although this is still a subject of ongoing research and debate.

Synchronicity and Dreamwork

When it comes to dreamwork, synchronicities offer a valuable lens through which to understand the practical and spiritual applications of our nocturnal visions. Here are some ways in which synchronicities manifest in relation to dreams:

1. **Premonitory Dreams:** Certain dreams appear to predict future events, and the unfolding of these events in real life can feel like a form of synchronicity. Though not fully understood, these kinds of dreams suggest an intriguing overlap between time, consciousness, and reality.

2. **Symbolic Resonance:** Often, symbols that appear in dreams also manifest in waking life shortly after the dream occurs. For example, you might dream of a white elephant, and the next day you stumble upon an article discussing the symbolism of white elephants in various cultures. This type of synchronicity can act as a confirmation or elaboration of the dream's message.

3. **Guidance and Decision-Making:** Synchronicities can

often provide guidance in decision-making processes. A dream could offer a particular direction or answer, which is then confirmed through synchronous events in waking life. This may be interpreted as the Universe or the Higher Self offering guidance.

4. **Emotional and Spiritual Growth:** Dreams can bring up unresolved issues or hidden aspects of the self. When these elements appear synchronistically in waking life, they often serve as triggers for emotional or spiritual growth.

By paying attention to these synchronicities, you enrich your dreamwork practice and open yourself to guidance from deeper layers of consciousness. These occurrences often invite you to look beyond the surface, encouraging you to explore the interplay between your internal landscape and the external world.

Practical Implications

The experience of synchronicity in the context of dreams necessitates a reflective approach to daily life. Keeping a dream journal gains added importance, as it allows you to track not only your dreams but also the synchronistic events that follow. This habit can serve as an essential tool for personal development and spiritual growth, acting as a feedback mechanism between your inner and outer worlds.

Moreover, sharing your experiences with trusted friends or in dream circles can further illuminate the patterns and meanings of these synchronicities. Often, the collective insight can offer new perspectives that were not apparent when you were dissecting the experiences alone.

When we consider the implications of synchronicities, we realize they offer more than mere interesting coincidences; they serve as gateways to a heightened form of awareness that integrates multiple dimensions of being. By weaving dreamwork and daily life experiences through the lens of synchronicity, we create a more holistic, interconnected view of reality that goes beyond the boundaries of conventional understanding.

Summary

Synchronicities offer a rich field of inquiry into the interconnected nature of dreams and waking life. Rooted in both historical and contemporary thought, the study of synchronicities equips us with an integrative approach to understanding our consciousness and the world around us. By tracking these meaningful coincidences through dream journals and reflective practices, we not only enrich our dreamwork but also open the door to deeper spiritual and emotional growth. Therefore, the role of synchronicities in dreams is not just a subject for intellectual curiosity but a path towards an enriched, interconnected experience of life itself.

CHAPTER 19: DREAM INCUBATION TECHNIQUES

Dream incubation is a fascinating area within the broader field of dream studies and dreamwork. Rooted in both historical practice and modern psychospiritual approaches, dream incubation involves setting an intention or posing a question before sleep in the hope of receiving guidance or insights from the dream world. This chapter delves into different methods of dream incubation, its psychological underpinnings, and how these techniques can be integrated into spiritual practices for personal growth and insight.

Historical Context of Dream Incubation

The concept of dream incubation is far from modern. Ancient civilizations like the Greeks and Egyptians placed immense significance on dreams as a means of divine communication. In ancient Egypt, "Dream Temples" dedicated to the god Serapis were established as centers for healing and guidance. Individuals would undergo purification rituals and then sleep within the temple precincts, hoping for a dream that would provide answers to their dilemmas or medical conditions. The Greeks also had their version of dream temples, known as Asclepieions, where they sought guidance from Asclepius, the god of medicine.

The practice of dream incubation in ancient times wasn't just a layman's endeavor; it was often facilitated by priests or religious figures well-versed in rituals to maximize the likelihood of significant dreams. These historical methods laid the groundwork for modern applications of dream incubation, often lending symbolic frameworks and ritualistic elements that many find helpful in the incubation process.

Techniques for Effective Dream Incubation

Dream incubation can range from simple to complex depending on the individual's preferences and the nature of the inquiry. Below are some techniques to consider:

Setting an Intention

Before going to sleep, it's essential to clarify what you're seeking from the dream. It can be a question you want answered, a decision you're trying to make, or even personal traits you wish to understand better. This intention can be as specific or as general as you'd like.

Physical Preparations

Some people find it useful to keep an object related to their question or intention by their bedside. This can be a photograph, a written note, or any symbolic item. Physically engaging with this object can serve to ground the intention more profoundly in the subconscious.

Mental and Emotional Preparations

For dream incubation to be most effective, your mind and emotions should be aligned with your intention. Meditation or deep relaxation techniques can serve to calm the mind, making it more receptive to the incubation process.

Journaling

Journaling your intention can lend it greater power and specificity. By writing it down, you solidify the intention in your conscious mind, increasing the chances that your subconscious will act on it.

Psychological Foundations of Dream Incubation

Psychologists like Carl Jung have suggested that the human mind is not just an individual repository of experiences but is also connected to a "collective unconscious," a well of archetypes and symbols common to all humanity. In this context, dream incubation can be seen as a method to tap into this vast reservoir for answers or guidance. Although not empirically proven, the idea lends an exciting dimension to dream incubation, blurring the lines between psychology and spirituality.

When viewed through a psychological lens, dream incubation can also be interpreted as a form of "directed dreaming," where the dreamer takes an active role in shaping the dreamscape. This control is not to be confused with lucid dreaming, where the dreamer is aware that they are dreaming while in the dream state. Instead, dream incubation works at the level of the subconscious, setting a stage for dreams to unfold.

Integrating Dream Incubation into Spiritual Practices

Dream incubation can effortlessly be integrated into broader spiritual practices. For example, those who engage in regular meditation can incorporate their dream intentions into their meditation routine. Alternatively, if you have a nightly ritual, adding a moment to articulate your dream intention can fortify the practice. In esoteric traditions like Kabbalah or Hermeticism, dream incubation might be part of a more extensive ritualistic framework, involving prayer, chanting, or visualization techniques. Regardless of your spiritual leanings, the principle remains the same: by setting a focused intention, you open up a channel of communication with the deeper layers of your consciousness, or perhaps even the divine, through the medium of dreams.

Summary

Dream incubation offers a compelling avenue for gaining insights and answers from the subconscious or potentially more profound spiritual realms. With roots in ancient religious practices and validated to some extent by psychological theories, dream incubation is a versatile tool for personal development and spiritual growth. By understanding its history, psychological underpinnings, and techniques, you can apply dream incubation in a manner that enriches your inner life and spiritual practice.

CHAPTER 20: NIGHTMARES AND SHADOW WORK

Dealing with the darker elements that appear in dreams

Dreams can serve as an illuminating lens into the hidden dimensions of our subconscious. While much attention is given to the favorable, enlightening aspects of dreaming, it is important to delve into the darker, often unsettling realms of nightmares and shadow elements. By engaging with these darker components, we can foster psychological growth and spiritual development. This chapter aims to dissect the concept of nightmares and how they relate to the process of shadow work in the context of dream interpretation.

Understanding Nightmares

Nightmares are vividly disturbing dreams that usually elicit emotions like fear, anxiety, or even terror. Contrary to popular belief, nightmares are not simply a manifestation of our deepest fears but can be interpreted as symbols representing unresolved issues or repressed emotions. It's essential to differentiate between nightmares that are random byproducts of stress or life events and those that carry significant symbolic weight. Nightmares could serve as an emotional or spiritual 'alarm clock,' signaling something in our lives that requires immediate attention.

The motifs in nightmares often come from our 'shadow self,' a term coined by Carl Jung to represent the darker, unconscious aspects of our personality that we either reject or are unaware of. These elements may include negative traits, hidden fears, or unacknowledged feelings. Nightmares may display these shadow elements through various symbols, scenarios, or even characters. An aggressive, monstrous figure in a nightmare might represent a repressed anger or a hidden aspect of yourself that you're uncomfortable acknowledging.

Shadow Work and Dream Interpretation

Shadow work involves confronting and integrating these darker aspects of ourselves into our conscious awareness. The process starts with identifying the shadow elements, which often make themselves known through the medium of nightmares. Dream journals can be incredibly useful for this practice, especially if you make a point to record nightmares as soon after waking as possible, to capture their visceral immediacy. One method for shadow work in dream interpretation involves the following steps:

1. **Identification**: Start by identifying recurring themes or symbols in your nightmares.
2. **Reflection**: Engage in a deep reflection to understand what these symbols might mean in the context of your life.
3. **Integration**: Take steps to confront and integrate these identified shadow aspects in your daily life.
4. **Dialogue**: Some practitioners recommend engaging in a mental dialogue with the shadow elements, treating them as separate entities with which you can negotiate

or reconcile.

5. **Action**: Take actionable steps, whether spiritual, psychological, or practical, to resolve the issues brought to light.

Ethical Considerations

When doing shadow work, especially as it relates to interpreting nightmares, there's an ethical dimension that should not be ignored. This process could stir deeply buried emotional traumas or psychological difficulties. Therefore, undertaking shadow work can be emotionally draining and should be approached with care. While many find this process enriching and emotionally liberating, others might need the support of a qualified therapist or spiritual guide. Always remember that shadow work is a deeply personal journey; you must consider your emotional and psychological threshold when navigating it.

In summary, nightmares and shadow work form an intricate web of psychological insights and spiritual lessons. Although nightmares can be unsettling, they offer a unique window into the hidden recesses of our subconscious, providing fertile ground for shadow work. Through the diligent interpretation of these darker elements, one can attain a more balanced, integrated self. By acknowledging and confronting the shadow, rather than banishing it to the unconscious, we enable a more holistic approach to spiritual development and self-awareness.

CHAPTER 21: DREAMS AND ASTRAL PROJECTION

The Connections Between Dreaming and Astral Travel or Out-of-Body Experiences

Dreaming, as a phenomenon that transcends the physical plane, inherently delves into metaphysical and spiritual territories. One such related domain is that of astral projection, often regarded as a form of out-of-body experience (OBE). Astral projection and OBEs hold a significant role in esoteric traditions and parapsychological studies alike, and many theorists suggest that there is a connective tissue between these experiences and the act of dreaming. In this chapter, we explore the relationships between dreams and astral projection, illuminating the theories, methods, and insights that link these two fascinating realms.

Similarities in Experience and Perception

At first glance, the experiential terrain of dreams and astral projection seems to share striking similarities. Both involve a departure from waking reality into an alternative space where conventional laws of physics and logic may not apply. This can include experiences such as flying, passing through walls, and observing oneself from a different vantage point.

In dreams, these actions are generally understood as symbolic representations of subconscious desires or fears. However, in the context of astral projection, they are often viewed as literal experiences occurring in a non-physical dimension called the "astral plane."

The emotions and sensations in both states also demonstrate resemblances. For example, an individual undergoing astral projection may experience feelings of tranquility, awe, or bliss, which are also common in certain dream states. Nevertheless, astral projection usually involves a conscious intent to venture into these realms, whereas dreams often happen spontaneously, lacking a predetermined agenda.

Theoretical Frameworks Connecting Dreams and Astral Projection

To comprehend the links between dreams and astral projection, one might delve into the foundations of esoteric traditions, spiritual teachings, and contemporary parapsychology. In Eastern philosophies, the concept of the "subtle body" provides a framework for understanding these phenomena. This subtle body is thought to separate from the physical form during astral projection and even during certain dream states, particularly lucid dreams. In Western occult traditions, astral projection is often described as an act of the "astral body" or the "etheric double" separating from the physical body and exploring different dimensions.

Psychologically, the concept of the "unconscious mind" acts as a potential bridge between these experiences. The unconscious is believed to be a reservoir of thoughts, memories, and experiences, some of which can manifest in dreams. In this context, astral projection could be considered an advanced form of dreaming where the individual retains a higher level of consciousness and volition, allowing them to explore this unconscious terrain with more awareness.

Practical Applications: Bridging Dreamwork and Astral Projection

For those interested in both dreamwork and astral projection, several methods can facilitate a deeper exploration of these interconnected realms. One such method is to employ techniques of lucid dreaming to transition into an astral projection. During a lucid dream, the dreamer realizes they are dreaming and gains a certain level of control over the dream narrative. At this point, advanced practitioners may use specific "exit techniques," such as imagining themselves floating upward, to shift from a lucid dream to an astral experience.

Journaling also remains a key practice for both dream and astral explorers. Recording one's experiences meticulously helps in recognizing patterns, themes, or symbols that may appear in both states. This can not only enrich the personal symbology but also create a more seamless integration of these diverse experiences into one's spiritual practice.

Moreover, meditation techniques that focus on body awareness can be employed to prime oneself for both dreaming and astral travel. These can include practices that bring awareness to one's breath, heartbeat, or energy centers (chakras), enabling an easier transition between states of consciousness.

In summary, while dreams and astral projection might appear as disparate experiences at first glance, they share significant conceptual, experiential, and methodological overlaps. The similarities in experience, coupled with overlapping theoretical frameworks, suggest that these states are interconnected facets of a broader metaphysical landscape. As our understanding deepens, the lines separating dreams from astral experiences may blur, revealing a unified field of consciousness exploration. The practical applications serve to bridge the gap between these two realms, enabling a more holistic approach to both dreamwork and astral travel.

CHAPTER 22: THE KABBALISTIC APPROACH TO DREAM INTERPRETATION

Introduction

The Kabbalistic tradition, a form of Jewish mysticism, offers a rich and nuanced perspective on the interpretation of dreams. Rooted in ancient wisdom, Kabbalah encompasses not just a religious or theological viewpoint but a metaphysical structure that seeks to explain the nature of God, the universe, and the human soul. Within this framework, dreams serve as a medium to access higher realms of consciousness and understanding. In this chapter, we delve into the ways in which the Kabbalistic approach interprets and values dreams, focusing on key concepts like Sefirot, the Tree of Life, and the Tetragrammaton.

Sefirot and the Tree of Life: The Foundation

The Tree of Life is a central symbol in Kabbalistic cosmology, representing the structure of reality itself. Comprised of ten spheres or "Sefirot," each sphere corresponds to a particular attribute of God and, by extension, a dimension of human experience and the cosmos. The Sefirot are connected by 22 paths, which coincide with the 22 letters of the Hebrew alphabet. In the context of dream interpretation, each Sefirot and its accompanying path offer a lens through which to explore the symbols and themes that emerge in dreams.

For instance, the Sefirah of "Chesed" represents mercy and kindness, and dreams that evoke these qualities could be thought of as stemming from or relating to this specific sphere. Conversely, "Gevurah" symbolizes severity or judgment; dreams invoking these feelings might be analyzed in the context of this Sefirah. The interconnected nature of the Sefirot suggests that dreams are rarely rooted in just one attribute but are instead a complex tapestry of interwoven themes and meanings.

Tetragrammaton: The Divine Name

In Kabbalistic thought, the name of God is more than a mere label; it is a formula that encapsulates the divine essence. The Tetragrammaton, often rendered as YHWH or Yahweh, is a four-lettered name of God that is considered too sacred to be spoken. Each letter in the Tetragrammaton is believed to correspond to a different level of reality, from the highest spiritual echelons to the material world we inhabit. Similarly, the letters are said to parallel levels of the human soul, from the "Nefesh" or life force to the "Yechidah," the singular essence of the soul.

When it comes to dreams, the Tetragrammaton provides a framework for understanding the multiple dimensions that may be at play. For instance, a dream featuring elements of material concern, such as work or money, could relate to the last "Heh" of YHWH, signifying the material realm. A dream filled with a sense of universal love or oneness might correspond to the "Yud" of YHWH, representing the highest spiritual realms. By examining dreams through the lens of the Tetragrammaton, one can glean insights into not just the dream's meaning but also its spiritual and existential significance.

Practical Application: Dreamwork in Kabbalistic Practice

Kabbalistic dream interpretation often involves a deep study of sacred texts, prayer, and meditative practices aimed at elevating consciousness. Dreams can be "decoded" through the Hebrew alphabet, assigning letters to symbols or themes and then evaluating these in the context of Kabbalistic wisdom. Furthermore, dreams that recur or are particularly vivid often prompt further mystical exploration. Kabbalistic sages have even devised specific prayers to be recited before sleep to invoke divine guidance in dreams.

Given the intricate symbolism and the multilayered approach to reality in Kabbalah, dream interpretation is rarely straightforward. It requires an integrated understanding of Kabbalistic principles, as well as an openness to exploring the profound and sometimes mysterious dimensions of the human psyche.

Summary

The Kabbalistic approach to dream interpretation offers a unique and multi-dimensional view into the realms of the subconscious. By utilizing the metaphysical constructs like the Sefirot and the Tree of Life, as well as the sacred Tetragrammaton, one can delve deeper into the labyrinthine corridors of dreams, gleaning both personal and universal insights. Like the practice of Kabbalah itself, Kabbalistic dreamwork is a continual journey—a transformative process that seeks to unify the individual soul with the ultimate divine source.

CHAPTER 23: DREAM YOGA AND TIBETAN PRACTICES

In this chapter, we delve into the intricate world of Tibetan Buddhism and its approach to dreams, particularly through the practice of Dream Yoga. This practice, rooted in the Vajrayana tradition, offers a transformative methodology to use the dream state as a conduit for spiritual enlightenment. Unlike many Western approaches to dreams, which often focus on interpretive or analytical methods, Dream Yoga emphasizes experiential wisdom and direct transformation of consciousness.

The Philosophical Foundations of Dream Yoga

The core of Dream Yoga is founded on Tibetan Buddhist philosophies, particularly those related to the nature of mind and reality. In Tibetan Buddhism, all phenomena, including dreams, are considered to be "empty" of inherent existence. They arise due to conditions and cease when those conditions change. This understanding brings a unique angle to dream interpretation. Rather than treating dream symbols as fixed or inherently meaningful, they are seen as constructs of the mind that can be deconstructed and understood in deeper, non-conceptual ways.

One of the foundational texts for Dream Yoga is the "Tibetan Book of the Dead" (Bardo Thodol), which outlines the experiences of the soul after death and during rebirth, describing various "bardos" or intermediate states. The dream state is considered one such bardo, making it a crucial aspect of Tibetan spiritual practice. By mastering the dream bardo, one can gain insights into other bardos, including the crucial moments of death and rebirth.

Practices and Techniques in Dream Yoga

Dream Yoga comprises several advanced techniques that go beyond mere dream recall or interpretation. It employs a multi-step approach that starts with basic practices and advances to more complex levels.

1. **Dream Recall**: The first step involves developing an acute awareness of one's dreams. Practitioners usually maintain a dream journal, much like in other forms of dreamwork, but the intention is not just to interpret the dream but to recognize its illusory nature.

2. **Lucidity**: The next step is achieving lucidity within the dream state. Lucid dreaming in this context is not just a phenomenon but a stepping stone to deeper spiritual experiences. Practitioners use specific mantras or visualization techniques to become conscious within their dreams.

3. **Transformation**: Once lucid, the practitioner engages in transforming dream objects or scenarios. For example, if one dreams of a fire, the practice may involve transforming it into water. This serves to underscore the illusory nature of dream phenomena and further detach from their seeming reality.

4. **Multiplying and Dissolving the Dream Body**: Advanced practices involve manipulating the

dreamer's own form within the dream. This includes multiplying the dream body and eventually dissolving it, symbolizing the dissolution of ego and the realization of emptiness.

5. **Union with the Deity**: In the most advanced stages, the practitioner visualizes merging with a deity or enlightened being, symbolizing the ultimate union of emptiness and form, or the merging of individual consciousness with universal awareness.

Applications in Spiritual Development

Dream Yoga is not an isolated practice but forms an integral part of a practitioner's overall spiritual regimen. Many Tibetan Buddhists incorporate these techniques as part of their daily meditation practices, often performing preparatory exercises before sleep to set the stage for Dream Yoga. These may include specific breathing exercises known as 'pranayama,' or visualizations designed to prepare the mind for lucid dreaming.

The ultimate aim of Dream Yoga is spiritual liberation, or 'enlightenment.' By consistently applying the methods of Dream Yoga, practitioners can loosen the grasp of egoic tendencies, become aware of the illusory nature of reality, and, in the most advanced stages, experience a non-dual state of awareness that transcends the dream/wake dichotomy. This awakened state, according to Tibetan teachings, is our natural condition but is usually obscured by the veils of ignorance and delusion.

In summary, Dream Yoga offers a rich and transformative approach to dreams, combining ancient wisdom with intricate techniques designed for spiritual evolution. Through the practice of Dream Yoga, one can use the dream state as a spiritual laboratory for testing and experiencing the profound philosophies of Tibetan Buddhism. This serves not only to deepen one's understanding of the dream state but also to foster spiritual growth and ultimate liberation.

CHAPTER 24: DREAMS AND DIVINATION

Introduction

Dreams have long been considered a fertile ground for mystical and spiritual exploration. Their elusive nature, combined with the profound experiences they offer, make dreams an area of particular intrigue when it comes to divination—the art and practice of seeking to gain insights into future events or hidden truths. The subject of this chapter is the intriguing intersection between dream interpretation and divinatory practices like Tarot, I Ching, and astrology. We'll delve into how these diverse practices can be integrated to provide richer, more comprehensive perspectives on both our waking and dream lives.

Dream Interpretation and Divination: A Symbiotic Relationship

At first glance, dream interpretation and divination may appear to be disparate practices. Dream interpretation focuses on the unconscious mind's expressions, primarily occurring during sleep, while divination is about probing the mystical or spiritual dimensions for wisdom, guidance, or predictive insights. However, upon closer inspection, the similarities become more evident.

Both practices serve as conduits for understanding deeper layers of reality, personal psyche, and even universal wisdom. They offer frameworks for making sense of the nebulous aspects of life—those things often outside the realm of rational thought or empirical evidence. For example, dream symbols can be as enigmatic as the imagery seen in Tarot cards. A dream of a crumbling tower could resonate well with the Tower card in a Tarot deck, symbolizing upheaval or significant change. Likewise, a recurring dream motif might find its counterpart in the I Ching as a hexagram, offering wisdom about balance or transformation.

This symbiosis can be particularly fruitful when you're confronted with a complex or multifaceted issue that eludes straightforward analysis. You could consult the Tarot for a general idea of the energies at play and then focus your intention on receiving a dream that provides further clarification. Or, a puzzling dream could be followed up with an astrological chart to discern the planetary alignments influencing your emotional or mental state.

Divinatory Practices and Their Integration into Dreamwork

Given the intricate relationship between dreams and divination, let's delve into how to integrate these two realms practically. Here are a few methods to consider:

Tarot and Dreams

One approach is to draw a Tarot card immediately upon waking from a significant dream. The imagery and symbolism of the card can provide a new lens through which to view the dream's content. For example, drawing the Moon card might emphasize the need to trust your intuition about a dream featuring a confusing maze or labyrinth.

I Ching and Dream Symbols

The I Ching, or Book of Changes, offers hexagrams—combinations of broken and unbroken lines—that are interpreted for their wisdom. After recording a dream, you can cast a hexagram to clarify its meaning. For instance, a dream of crossing a river might be augmented by a hexagram signifying 'Obstruction' or 'Deliverance,' offering a more nuanced understanding of the dream's implications.

Astrology and Dream Phases

Astrology provides a macrocosmic view of individual experiences. Understanding the current planetary transits can illuminate the quality and subject matter of your dreams. For instance, a Mars transit over your natal Moon could coincide with dreams of conflict or aggression. Knowing this astrological influence can add an additional layer of interpretation.

Summary

Dreams and divinatory practices like Tarot, I Ching, and astrology can be seamlessly combined to offer enriched perspectives on the challenges and mysteries of life. While each has its own unique framework and methodology, their intersection provides a fertile ground for deeper understanding and spiritual growth. By engaging with these ancient practices, one can forge a more integrated path towards self-awareness and personal transformation, illuminated by the intricate dance of the unconscious mind and the divine.

CHAPTER 25: DREAM SYMBOLS IN SACRED GEOMETRY

Sacred geometry is a fascinating area of study that explores the mathematical and geometric aspects of the universe as a key to understanding the divine order of existence. It posits that certain shapes and figures have sacred meanings and that they appear consistently in nature, architecture, and even our dreams. As we dive into the realm of intermediate-level dream interpretation, it is important to explore how these geometric shapes may hold profound insights into the metaphysical aspects of our dream lives.

The Foundations of Sacred Geometry

Sacred geometry isn't a new concept; it has ancient roots stretching back to the philosophical schools of Pythagoras, Plato, and even earlier civilizations like Egypt and Mesopotamia. The basic premise lies in the belief that geometry and mathematics are not just tools for measurement but are also keys to understanding the mysteries of existence. Shapes like the circle, square, and triangle are more than just simple geometric figures; they are archetypes imbued with deep metaphysical significance.

In sacred geometry, shapes often build upon each other to form more complex structures. For example, the Vesica Piscis, a shape created by the overlap of two circles, is considered to be a symbol of the union of opposites. The Flower of Life, a complex figure made up of multiple overlapping circles, is believed to represent the cycle of creation, encompassing life, death, and rebirth.

Sacred Geometry in Dreams

Dreams are a rich canvas where the complexities of our psyche find expression. Sacred geometric shapes often make their appearance in the dream realm, and their interpretations can offer fresh insights into our inner worlds. For example, dreaming of a spiral, which in sacred geometry is associated with evolution and growth, might indicate a personal journey toward self-improvement or enlightenment. A hexagon, related to the structure of organic compounds and beehives, could symbolize community, work, and interconnectedness.

It is worth noting that these shapes may appear in various forms within the dreamscape. They could be the design of a building, the pattern of a carpet, or even the formation of people or stars. The context in which they appear is also essential for a nuanced understanding. For example, a square could indicate stability or confinement depending on other elements present in the dream.

Practical Application: Interpreting Geometric Symbols in Dreams

Interpreting sacred geometric symbols in dreams involves a multi-faceted approach. First, take note of the symbol's general meaning within the framework of sacred geometry. For instance, a triangle often symbolizes harmony and divinity as it has three sides, which in numerology is a sacred number.

Next, consider the context in which the symbol appears. If a dream involves climbing a spiral staircase, the act of climbing adds another layer of meaning to the spiral's inherent symbolism of growth or evolution. This could signify an upward trajectory in some aspect of your life, perhaps spiritual or career-wise.

Finally, integrate this interpretation with the overall theme and other symbols in the dream to arrive at a comprehensive understanding. Personal associations with the shapes also matter. Your own cultural background, personal experiences, and current life circumstances can tailor the universal meanings these shapes carry.

Summary

Sacred geometry opens a new dimension of understanding our dreams by linking them to universal patterns and principles. The ancient wisdom encapsulated in geometric shapes like circles, spirals, and hexagons provides a richer vocabulary for deciphering the complex language of our dreamscapes. By applying this layer of interpretation, we not only gain deeper insights into our inner worlds but also touch upon the mystical, unifying threads that connect us to the cosmos.

CHAPTER 26: DREAMS AND THE CYCLE OF LIFE: BIRTH, DEATH, REBIRTH

Dreams are not merely nocturnal vignettes; they are a symbolic language deeply interwoven with the entire fabric of our existence. One of the most potent arenas where dreams play an extraordinary role is in the cyclical processes of life—birth, death, and rebirth. These profound transitions in human life not only arouse emotional upheaval but also kindle a spate of dream activities. Such dreams often seem more vivid, more urgent, and are usually imbued with symbols that are both universally significant and deeply personal. This chapter delves into how dreams intersect with these major life transitions, the archetypal symbols often encountered, and the potential for spiritual enrichment.

Birth: The Advent of Life

The process of birth is not just a physical event but also a deeply spiritual one, encompassing not just the individual being born but also the parents, especially the mother. Dreams during pregnancy often consist of potent archetypal imagery such as water, emergence, and the Earth Mother. These are believed to be indicative of the immense transformation a woman undergoes, akin to a rebirth of her own identity. Similarly, prospective fathers may dream of protective figures or symbols of strength, echoing archetypal paternal roles.

Childbirth is a transformative experience, and many cultures believe that dreams can offer premonitions or guidance. For example, some indigenous tribes consider dreams during pregnancy to be prophecies about the unborn child's future, attributes, or challenges. In more modern settings, people may report dreams that eerily seem to predict the gender of the child or foreshadow pregnancy complications. While such prophetic dreams aren't universally accepted, their frequency during these times of transition is noteworthy.

Death: The Great Unknown

Death, like birth, is another liminal state where the veil between ordinary reality and the mystical appears to thin, often activating vivid and poignant dreams for the dying and their loved ones. For the dying, dreams often include deceased relatives or serene landscapes, potentially providing comfort or even facilitating a smoother transition to the afterlife. There's a wealth of anecdotal evidence suggesting that such dreams can significantly impact a dying person's emotional well-being. In the realm of Jungian psychology, these can be seen as the manifestation of archetypes like the Wise Old Man or the Eternal Mother, signaling a return to the collective unconscious.

For the grieving, dreams can serve as a continuation of their relationship with the deceased. These dreams often bring messages of reassurance or resolution and may even serve as a form of closure. While skeptics might attribute this to the brain processing grief, many spiritual traditions view such dreams as legitimate communications from the afterlife.

Rebirth: The Cycle Continues

The concept of rebirth is entrenched in various religious and spiritual traditions, from Hinduism's belief in reincarnation to Christianity's concept of resurrection. Dreams often play a role in the individual's understanding of this cyclical process. These are often transformative dreams that feature archetypal symbols like the Phoenix, the Ouroboros (snake eating its tail), or the Wheel of Fortune, signifying endless cycles of destruction and renewal.

In psychological terms, dreams featuring rebirth may be seen as the mind's way of signaling that an individual is going through a psychological transformation or paradigm shift. This could be something as tangible as a career change or as ethereal as a shift in spiritual beliefs. In both cases, the dream serves as a metaphorical platform for an internal metamorphosis, often guiding or even accelerating the process.

Conclusion

Dreams serve as a reflective mirror, magnifying our internal landscapes, especially during times of immense change such as birth, death, and theoretical rebirth. They offer an opportunity for deep spiritual insights and can act as navigational aids during these transitional phases. The archetypal symbols and scenarios that populate these dreams serve as shared cultural and psychological markers, bridging the individual experience with universal truths. Understanding the nature and symbology of dreams during these crucial life events can open up avenues for personal growth, spiritual enrichment, and even provide comfort in times of uncertainty and loss.

CHAPTER 27: DREAM TELEPATHY AND SHARED DREAMING

Dreams have long been viewed as a mysterious realm where the boundaries of time, space, and individuality blur. At an intermediate level of understanding, one of the most intriguing areas of dream research is the phenomenon of dream telepathy and shared dreaming. These occurrences challenge the conventional ideas of consciousness being confined to an individual's mind and suggest a collective or interconnected dimension.

Dream Telepathy: A Controversial Subject

Dream telepathy is a contentious topic within both scientific and spiritual communities. In these instances, it appears that information or emotional states are transferred between people without the use of conventional senses. Often, one person dreams of something specific concerning another person—information they had no way of knowing through regular means. While science struggles to find empirical evidence supporting the existence of dream telepathy, countless anecdotal accounts attest to its reality. Historically, indigenous cultures and spiritual traditions have widely accepted the notion that dreams can serve as a medium for extrasensory communication.

Several experiments, often criticized for their lack of stringent controls, have nevertheless attempted to investigate dream telepathy. In these experiments, a "sender" concentrates on a particular image or concept while the "receiver" sleeps and subsequently dreams. The receiver's dreams are then analyzed to see if they incorporate the image or concept that the sender was focusing on. Although not universally accepted, some studies do indicate a higher-than-chance occurrence of shared elements between the sender's thoughts and the receiver's dreams.

Shared Dreaming: Beyond Coincidence?

Shared dreaming is another phenomenon that puzzles dream researchers and enthusiasts alike. In these scenarios, two or more individuals report having the same or strikingly similar dreams during the same timeframe. These dreams can be identical in detail or share thematic elements, characters, or symbols. Unlike dream telepathy, where one person appears to receive information from another, shared dreaming suggests a mutual experience of the same dream landscape. This has led some scholars to ponder if such dreams occur within a "shared psychic space" and what the implications of this might be for our understanding of collective consciousness.

Several theories attempt to explain the phenomenon of shared dreaming. Jung's concept of the collective unconscious argues that there is a repository of archetypes and symbols shared by all humans, potentially giving rise to similar dream content. Other explanations veer into the realm of quantum physics, speculating that entangled minds could account for shared experiences. Lastly, the metaphysical community often looks towards the idea of astral planes, a shared spiritual space where these dreams could theoretically occur.

Integrating Dream Telepathy and Shared Dreaming into Spiritual Practices

While empirical evidence may be scant, for those who experience dream telepathy or shared dreaming, the phenomena are deeply significant. Such experiences often serve as catalysts for deeper spiritual exploration. Dream journals can be particularly illuminating, capturing the nuances of shared dreams or telepathic experiences for later analysis and integration into one's spiritual path. Practitioners of meditation and mindfulness find that these disciplines can heighten the frequency and clarity of such dreams, possibly by increasing mental and spiritual attunement.

In spiritual circles, these phenomena are often explored in dream groups where individuals share and analyze their dreams collectively. The objective is not only to gain personal insights but also to understand how dreams can serve as conduits for interconnectedness. Moreover, some spiritual traditions offer guided practices aimed at intentionally cultivating telepathic or shared dreams, often under the guidance of a knowledgeable mentor.

Summary

The subjects of dream telepathy and shared dreaming challenge our conventional understandings of individual consciousness and open up intriguing possibilities for interconnectedness. While these phenomena remain controversial and incompletely understood, they continue to be areas of active research and discussion. For many, they also offer a gateway to deeper spiritual exploration and understanding, inviting us to look beyond the boundaries of our individual selves to something much more collective and interconnected.

CHAPTER 28: DREAMS IN THE ALCHEMICAL TRADITION

The intersection of dreams and the alchemical tradition presents a labyrinthine landscape that beckons for closer examination. While alchemy is often associated with the material endeavor of transmuting base metals into gold, its esoteric dimensions are deeply concerned with spiritual transformation. Dreams, which we've explored in various contexts earlier in this book, serve as a compelling domain where the alchemical processes manifest symbolically. In this chapter, we delve into how these alchemical symbols and processes appear in dreams, illuminating pathways toward inner transformation.

Alchemical Symbols in Dreams

Alchemical symbols such as the Ouroboros (snake eating its tail), the Philosopher's Stone, or the merging of opposites (Sol and Luna, for instance) are recurring motifs in alchemical literature. When they appear in dreams, they are often indicative of transformative processes taking place within the unconscious mind.

The Ouroboros

The Ouroboros often symbolizes the cyclic nature of life, death, and rebirth. Its appearance in a dream could signify a time of personal renewal or the completion of a life phase. The circular shape also echoes the Jungian concept of individuation, a process of becoming the person you are inherently meant to be.

The Philosopher's Stone

In alchemical tradition, the Philosopher's Stone is the pinnacle of achievement, representing both material abundance and spiritual enlightenment. When this symbol appears in dreams, it can signify the nearing completion of a long journey of self-discovery or the realization of a life purpose.

Sol and Luna

Sol and Luna represent the alchemical archetypes of the Sun and the Moon, often denoting the masculine and feminine principles. When these appear in dreams, they can signify the need for balance or integration of opposites within the psyche.

Alchemical Processes as Dream Narratives

Alchemical transformation is usually delineated in stages, each comprising specific processes like calcination, dissolution, coagulation, and sublimation, among others. These processes can serve as metaphorical frameworks for interpreting dreams, which often encapsulate similar themes of breakdown, dissolution, and rebuilding.

Calcination and Dissolution

In alchemy, calcination involves the heating of a substance until it turns to ash, symbolizing the destruction of the ego or false self. Dissolution is the subsequent process where the remnants are dissolved in liquid, indicating further breakdown of old structures. Dreams that involve scenes of destruction—be it a burning house or the crumbling of an edifice—could be understood as analogous to these alchemical processes, signifying necessary stages of breakdown before rebuilding can occur.

Coagulation and Sublimation

Coagulation symbolizes the reformation of the Self, often represented by the Philosopher's Stone. Sublimation refers to the spiritualization of matter, ascending from the material to the ethereal. Dreams of rebirth, ascending mountains, or even the birth of a child could correspond to these processes, symbolizing a transformative realization or a renewed sense of purpose.

Alchemy as a Bridge to Spiritual Transformation

In historical context, alchemy serves as a precursor to modern psychology and was deeply embedded in spiritual traditions. Medieval alchemists were often spiritual seekers who viewed the transmutation of base metals into gold as a metaphor for spiritual enlightenment. Similarly, modern dreamwork can be viewed as a continuation of these age-old practices, offering roadmaps to navigate the complexities of the inner world.

By applying alchemical symbolism and processes to dream interpretation, you're essentially continuing a tradition that has its roots in the most ancient mystical practices. The symbols and processes not only enrich our understanding of the dream narratives but also provide a robust framework for personal transformation.

In summary, alchemy and dreams share a metaphorical language rich in symbols and processes that articulate the ineffable dimensions of transformation—both material and spiritual. Recognizing and decoding these symbols within your dreams can serve as stepping stones toward greater self-awareness and, ultimately, spiritual transcendence. This chapter has hopefully provided you with insightful tools to integrate alchemical symbolism into your dreamwork, elevating it from mere interpretation to a transformative spiritual practice.

CHAPTER 29: INTERPRETING PARADOXICAL AND ILLOGICAL DREAM ELEMENTS

Introduction

Dreams often present us with elements that seem illogical or paradoxical. While earlier chapters have delved into the interpretation of more straightforward dream symbols and situations, this chapter aims to shed light on these challenging, yet intrinsically meaningful, aspects of dreaming. Such elements often defy rational analysis but can yield rich insights when approached with an open mind and a nuanced understanding of dream logic.

Dream Logic Versus Waking Logic

In waking life, our thoughts and perceptions are generally guided by what we consider to be logic or rationality. This logical framework, however, often gets suspended or altered in the dream state. For example, you might find yourself flying in a dream or walking through walls—actions that defy the laws of physics but feel entirely plausible within the context of the dream.

It's essential to understand that dream logic operates on a different set of principles. The renowned psychologist Carl Jung suggested that the dream state engages with our unconscious mind, which does not operate under the same constraints as our conscious, waking mind. While waking logic is linear and bound by the laws of cause and effect, dream logic is more fluid, allowing for paradoxes and contradictions to coexist. When interpreting dreams, adopting an approach that respects this different logical framework can be immensely helpful. Embrace the surreal and the absurd as carriers of messages, rather than anomalies to be dismissed.

The Role of Paradoxes in Dream Interpretation

Paradoxical elements in dreams can be unsettling but are also ripe for exploration. A paradox, by definition, is a situation or statement that seems to contradict itself yet might be true. In dreams, paradoxes may manifest in various forms, such as impossible geometries, characters who are simultaneously two different people, or sequences of events that defy linear time.

These paradoxes often challenge our waking understanding of the world but can serve as potent symbols for complex emotional or spiritual states. For instance, a dream in which you are both the pursuer and the pursued could signify an internal conflict or dual feelings about a particular situation. Similarly, a dream featuring a Möbius strip— a surface with only one side and one boundary—could symbolize an eternal cycle or a situation where beginnings and endings merge.

Dream paradoxes also echo some of the essential themes in spirituality and mysticism, such as the coexistence of opposites in a unified whole. In Eastern philosophies like Taoism, this is exemplified by the concept of Yin and Yang, which represents the interconnectedness of seemingly opposite or contrary forces. In dream analysis, paradoxical elements often point towards a need for synthesis, integration, or the acceptance of ambiguity and complexity in one's waking life.

Strategies for Navigating Illogical Dream Elements

When confronted with illogical or absurd elements in dreams, it can be tempting to either dismiss them as nonsensical or force them into a rational framework. However, doing so risks missing out on valuable insights. Instead, consider the following strategies:

1. **Embrace Ambiguity**: Accept that the dream element may not have a single, clear-cut meaning. Sometimes, the very essence of the symbol lies in its ambiguity.

2. **Contextual Analysis**: Examine the illogical element in the context of the entire dream and your current life situations. An absurdity in a dream may make perfect emotional sense when viewed against your waking experiences or emotional state.

3. **Multi-layered Interpretation**: Recognize that dream symbols can operate on multiple levels simultaneously. A flying pig might represent an impossibility in one context, a desire for freedom in another, and an omen of unexpected events in yet another.

4. **Engage with the Symbol**: Sometimes, actively engaging with a paradoxical or illogical dream element in subsequent dreams or in meditative visualizations can lead to more clarity. You might ask the symbol what it represents or why it has appeared to you.

5. **Consult Multiple Perspectives**: While your own

intuition is paramount, sometimes discussing the dream with trusted friends or advisors who are well-versed in dream interpretation can offer new perspectives on the illogical elements.

Summary

Dreams often contain elements that defy waking logic, presenting us with paradoxes, contradictions, and absurdities. Rather than dismissing these as meaningless, we can embrace the different logic that governs the dream realm. By employing thoughtful strategies, we can decode these complex symbols to gain valuable insights into our emotional and spiritual lives. The key is to approach them with an open mind and a willingness to delve into the intricate tapestry of meanings they may contain.

CHAPTER 30: SLEEP DISORDERS AND THEIR IMPACT ON DREAMING

Introduction

As we delve further into the mystical dimensions of dreams, we must also give due consideration to the biological and psychological aspects of our nocturnal visions. Sleep disorders can considerably impact both the quality and content of our dreams, shaping our dream landscape in specific ways that might not be immediately obvious. In this chapter, we will examine some of the most common sleep disorders, their characteristics, and how they influence our dream experiences.

Sleep Disorders and Dream Disruptions

Insomnia

Insomnia, characterized by difficulty falling asleep or staying asleep, poses a significant barrier to entering the dream state. Given that dreams typically occur during REM (Rapid Eye Movement) sleep, a phase that becomes increasingly prolonged and vivid as the night progresses, insomnia truncates these opportunities. Therefore, someone suffering from insomnia might not only experience reduced dreaming but may also have difficulty recalling any dreams that they do have. Additionally, the stress and anxiety often accompanying insomnia can manifest as tense or anxiety-filled dream scenarios.

Sleep Apnea

Sleep apnea is a condition in which a person's breathing is interrupted during sleep. This constant disruption impacts the sleep cycle, often preventing the individual from reaching or maintaining REM sleep, where most vivid dreaming occurs. The fragmented sleep experience can lead to dreams that feel disjointed or nonsensical, making dream interpretation a challenging task. There's also a predilection for more nightmarish dreams due to the physical distress experienced.

Narcolepsy

Narcolepsy, a neurological condition characterized by extreme sleepiness during waking hours and sudden bouts of sleep, has a unique influence on dreaming. Those with narcolepsy often enter REM sleep almost immediately upon falling asleep, bypassing the usual progression of sleep stages. As a result, they might experience unusually vivid and frequent dreams. There are even instances where the vivid dream content may blend with waking reality, creating hallucinatory experiences that can be both mystical and disorienting.

Parasomnias

Parasomnias are a category of sleep disorders involving unwanted events or experiences that occur while falling asleep, sleeping, or waking up. Examples include sleepwalking, night terrors, and REM sleep behavior disorder. In terms of dreams, parasomnias often result in dreams that are acted out physically to some extent, making the line between dream and reality more ambiguous. Sleepwalking, for example, may correspond with dreams of movement or travel. Night terrors are usually accompanied by frightening dream content, though the individual may not always remember the dream upon waking.

The Dialectics of Dreams and Sleep Disorders

While sleep disorders undeniably affect dreams, the relationship is not entirely one-sided. Dreams themselves can be therapeutic mediums to explore the emotional and psychological aspects of sleep disorders. Many individuals have reported gaining insights into their conditions through their dream content, and some even find solutions or coping mechanisms through dreamwork. Therefore, understanding the ways sleep disorders affect dreams can also offer a pathway for self-reflection and potentially some level of therapeutic intervention.

Dream therapy, a subset of psychotherapy, has been increasingly used to treat sleep disorders like insomnia. By exploring the dream narratives and symbols, therapists and individuals may unearth underlying fears, anxieties, or unresolved conflicts that exacerbate sleep issues. However, it's essential to consult healthcare professionals for accurate diagnosis and treatment options.

Summary

Sleep disorders significantly impact the quality, frequency, and content of dreams. Conditions like insomnia, sleep apnea, narcolepsy, and parasomnias each present unique disruptions to the dream landscape, affecting not just the structure of dreams but also their interpretive value. However, dreams are not merely passive recipients of these influences; they can also serve as lenses through which the ramifications of these disorders are explored and understood. As we continue our journey into the deeper recesses of dream interpretation, awareness of the physiological aspects is crucial for a comprehensive understanding of our dreamscapes.

CHAPTER 31: QUANTUM DREAMING: THE FRONTIERS OF DREAM SCIENCE

Introduction

In the ever-evolving landscape of dream studies, few domains are as speculative, controversial, yet tantalizing as the interface between quantum mechanics and the phenomenology of dreaming. By peeling back the layers of dream states and applying principles from quantum mechanics, researchers and theorists attempt to bridge the gap between two ostensibly disparate realms: the oneiric world of dreams and the infinitesimal ballet of quantum particles. This chapter navigates the intricate mazes of quantum mechanics and how its principles might help elucidate the enigmatic world of dreaming.

Quantum Mechanics: A Brief Primer

Quantum mechanics, at its core, is a branch of physics that

attempts to explain the behavior of matter and energy at subatomic scales. One of its seminal ideas is the principle of superposition, which posits that a quantum system can exist in multiple states simultaneously. The famous "Schrödinger's cat" thought experiment, which suggests that a cat could be both alive and dead until observed, serves as a metaphorical illustration of this principle.

Another significant concept in quantum theory is entanglement, the phenomenon where the states of two particles are inextricably linked, irrespective of the distance that separates them. The "spooky action at a distance," as Einstein called it, challenges our conventional understanding of space-time and locality.

The Quantum-Dream Hypothesis

Applying the principles of quantum mechanics to dreams can at first seem like a stretch, but some parallels are too compelling to ignore. For example, the superposition principle might be invoked to explain the often fluid, paradoxical, and multi-layered nature of dreams. Just as a quantum particle can exist in various states simultaneously, dream elements can defy linear logic and present multiple scenarios at the same time. This correlates with some of the phenomena observed in dreaming, where contradictory events, settings, or interpretations coexist.

Entanglement could potentially offer an explanation for phenomena like shared dreaming or dream telepathy. If the dream states of two individuals could be entangled in a manner similar to quantum particles, it would theoretically be possible for both to experience the same dream, or at least interconnected elements within their respective dreams, irrespective of physical distance.

Moreover, quantum mechanics may offer a basis for understanding how dreams interact with the conscious mind.

The act of remembering a dream could be seen as analogous to the "collapse" of a quantum wave function—the transition from multiple possibilities to a single observed reality. In other words, the dream exists in a superposition of all its possible meanings until it is observed or remembered, at which point it takes on a specific form.

Skepticism and Future Directions

It's important to note that the quantum-dream hypothesis is still largely theoretical and has its fair share of skeptics. Critics often point out that the brain operates at a macroscopic level, far removed from the scale at which quantum mechanics plays a role. Additionally, there's the "woo-woo" factor: the risk of reducing quantum mechanics to a mystical catch-all explanation for inexplicable phenomena.

However, the intersection between quantum theory and dreams remains a burgeoning field, full of promise and intrigue. As technology advances, we might develop the tools necessary to probe these ideas more concretely. For instance, quantum computing could potentially model complex brain processes, including dream states, at the quantum level, providing insights that classical computing can't.

Summary

The frontier of quantum dreaming is a hazy horizon that tantalizes both scientists and dream enthusiasts alike. By applying quantum principles like superposition and entanglement, theorists seek to elucidate the fluid, paradoxical, and sometimes collective experiences of dreaming. Although speculative and fraught with controversy, this area of study opens up exciting avenues for future research and understanding. Like quantum particles that exist in a realm of endless possibilities until observed, the quantum-dream hypothesis itself awaits rigorous scrutiny, promising to either revolutionize our understanding of dreams or remain a tantalizing enigma.

CHAPTER 32: LUCID DREAMING AS A SPIRITUAL PRACTICE

Lucid dreaming, where the dreamer becomes aware that they are dreaming while still immersed in the dream, offers profound opportunities for spiritual growth. This advanced chapter will delve into techniques for achieving and utilizing lucid dreams in the context of spiritual practice. The focus will be on expanding awareness, seeking transcendent experiences, and harnessing the transformative power of lucid dreaming.

Techniques for Achieving Lucidity

Achieving lucidity often requires deliberate preparation and a certain level of expertise in dreamwork. Here are some advanced methods you may wish to explore:

1. **Dream Sign Recognition**: Unlike basic dream journaling, this involves a deep analysis of recurring elements or "dream signs" that commonly appear in your dreams. Identifying these could act as a trigger for lucidity.

2. **Wake Back To Bed (WBTB)**: In this method, you interrupt your sleep cycle intentionally to awaken your mind. After staying awake for a short period, perhaps 15 to 30 minutes, you return to sleep,

increasing the likelihood of entering a lucid dream.

3. **Mnemonic Induction of Lucid Dreams (MILD)**: As you drift off to sleep, you concentrate on a mnemonic or affirmation to remind yourself that you will recognize you're dreaming. This is coupled with the visualization of a recent dream, changing its outcome in your imagination to one where you become lucid.

4. **Advanced Reality Checks**: Beyond common reality checks like finger-counting or nose-pinching, you can incorporate more complex intellectual tasks. For instance, questioning the nature of your surroundings in a Socratic manner can serve as a higher-order reality check, more potent in inducing lucidity.

Spiritual Goals in Lucid Dreaming

Once you have gained the ability to become lucid consistently, you can begin to apply this awareness toward spiritual ends. Here are some pathways to consider:

1. **Self-Inquiry and Inner Exploration**: Being lucid grants you an opportunity to directly interact with elements of your subconscious mind. You can ask dream characters or even the dream itself profound questions about your spiritual path, personal traumas, or deep-seated fears.

2. **Sacred Geometry and Mystical Experiences**: Lucid dreaming provides a vivid and interactive space to explore complex geometrical shapes like the Flower of Life or the Sri Yantra. Immersing yourself in these shapes can potentially lead to profound mystical experiences.

3. **Transpersonal and Ancestral Connection**: In a lucid state, it's possible to seek encounters with archetypal

figures, spirit guides, or ancestors. These interactions can offer guidance and can be transformational in nature.

4. **Practicing Compassion and Altruism**: Lucid dreams can be an experimental ground for practicing virtues. One can engage in compassionate activities within the dream, affecting not just the dream characters but also potentially fostering these virtues in waking life.

Integration into Wider Spiritual Practice

Lucid dreaming should not be an isolated endeavor but integrated into your broader spiritual practice. Here are some points to consider:

1. **Meditative Synergy**: Practices like mindfulness and transcendental meditation can be applied within a lucid dream to deepen the state of lucidity and enhance spiritual realization.

2. **Scripture and Mantra Recitation**: Within a lucid dream, you can engage in the recitation of spiritual texts or mantras. This provides an unparalleled opportunity for internalization, as the dream state is highly receptive to imprinting.

3. **Astrological Correspondences**: You can align your lucid dreaming practice with astrological events, such as full moons, eclipses, or planetary transits. This helps to harmonize your internal dream landscape with external cosmic energies, adding another layer of meaning and depth.

4. **Ritual Integration**: Whether it's a daily prayer, a series of yoga poses, or a set sequence of breathwork, your lucid dreaming experience can be both a subject and object of these rituals, thereby enriching both the

dream state and the ritual itself.

In sum, lucid dreaming offers more than just recreational escapism or psychological insight; it offers a direct, experiential pathway for spiritual growth. The methods to attain lucidity are numerous and the ways to apply this state toward spiritual ends are only limited by your own imagination and intent. As such, lucid dreaming stands as a robust, multifaceted discipline within the greater sphere of dreamwork, ripe for explorative ventures into the realms of the spirit.

CHAPTER 33: TIME AND DREAMS: THE TEMPORAL DIMENSION

Dreams have been a subject of fascination for millennia, provoking both scholarly examination and mystical contemplation. A particularly engrossing aspect of dreams is their relationship with time. This chapter delves into the intricate terrain of time's behavior in the dream state, exploring its malleability, non-linearity, and the associated metaphysical and psychological implications.

Temporal Fluidity in Dreams

Time in dreams doesn't abide by the rigid structure we're accustomed to in waking life. Seconds can stretch into minutes, or even hours, while significant events may flash by in an instant. This fluidity has intrigued philosophers, psychologists, and neuroscientists alike, posing questions about the subjectivity of time experience. From the psychological perspective, the feeling of extended time in dreams may be attributable to the activation of different areas of the brain responsible for temporal judgment during the REM (Rapid Eye Movement) phase of sleep. Meanwhile, metaphysical theories often equate the dream world's temporal fluidity with higher planes of existence where time is but a construct, giving us glimpses into eternal or cyclical conceptions of time.

Time Loops and Non-Linearity

In the dream state, the linearity of time frequently breaks down. Events may occur out of sequence, looping or reversing in a way that defies the "arrow of time" that dominates our waking reality. Even more striking are precognitive dreams, where events are dreamt before they occur in waking life, though such claims often invite scientific skepticism. The fascinating aspect here is that these instances challenge our typical understanding of causality. Could it be that our dreaming mind taps into a 'timeless' dimension where past, present, and future co-exist? Or perhaps, these experiences are distortions of our cognitive functions, whereby our mind rearranges memories and anticipations into a non-linear narrative.

Dreams as Time Travel

Some dream explorers report experiences that can only be described as time travel, encountering historical or even futuristic settings with convincing detail. While it's tempting to attribute such dreams to an expansive collective unconscious or even to metaphysical realms, one must consider the role of individual psychology. The mind is a treasure trove of knowledge, memories, and cultural inputs. It could construct historically or futuristically accurate settings by piecing together data from books, movies, and subconscious archetypes. Then again, philosophically speaking, if time is but an illusion, as some Eastern philosophies suggest, the concept of time travel in dreams could be a mundane point in a reality where time is but a labyrinth of eternal nows.

The enigmatic relationship between time and dreams opens a wealth of avenues for exploration. Whether viewed through the lens of psychology, neuroscience, metaphysics, or spirituality, the dream world's fluid and often nonlinear conception of time challenges our most fundamental assumptions about reality. While our understanding remains inchoate and speculative, these curiosities catalyze interdisciplinary dialogues that can enrich both scientific research and spiritual practices. By venturing to explore the nexus of time and dreams, we not only gain a deeper understanding of dream phenomena but may also unlock new ways of conceptualizing time itself, contributing to broader discussions in philosophy, physics, and consciousness studies.

CHAPTER 34: THE SHAMANIC JOURNEY: DREAMS AS SPIRITUAL QUESTS

The realm of shamanic journeying has long captivated the imagination and spirituality of numerous cultures worldwide. Through particular rituals and states of consciousness, shamans travel between worlds to gain wisdom, healing, and transformative insights. This chapter delves into the intricate relationship between dreams and shamanic journeys, examining how one can view dreams as spiritual quests that align with shamanic practices.

Dreams as Journeys Between Worlds

In shamanic traditions, the journey between worlds is not merely metaphorical but a real experience. Shamans transition from ordinary reality to non-ordinary reality by altering their state of consciousness through drumming, fasting, dancing, or the use of entheogens. Within this altered state, they can interact with spirits, retrieve lost soul parts, or gain insights into personal and community issues. Likewise, in dreams, we find ourselves effortlessly navigating different realms—sometimes familiar, sometimes bizarre, and sometimes ineffably transcendent. The architecture of the dream state allows us to interact with elements that might be considered "otherworldly" or numinous. These experiences can have therapeutic or transformative potential, often paralleling shamanic soul journeys.

Rituals and Symbols in Dreams and Shamanic Practices

The role of ritual is paramount in shamanic practices. Rituals prepare the mind and body for a transformative experience and provide a structured framework for interacting with the spiritual realm. In dreams, we often encounter ritualistic elements, be it in the form of ceremonial dances, rites of passage, or symbol-laden scenarios. These ritualistic elements in dreams can serve as a call to engage more deeply with the spiritual dimension of our lives.

Similarly, the presence of potent symbols in both dreams and shamanic journeys is striking. Animals, in particular, are significant. In shamanic tradition, they often appear as spirit guides or totems that offer wisdom or protection. Dreams frequently feature animals as archetypal symbols or guides. Recognizing the symbology can offer a deeper understanding of one's spiritual journey.

Additionally, certain symbolic objects often recur in both shamanic journeys and dreams—items such as feathers, stones, or ritualistic implements like drums or rattles. These can serve as markers or tools for the spiritual quest, their appearance in dreams signaling that one is on a journey of significant spiritual depth.

Techniques for Integrating Dreams and Shamanic Journeying

For those interested in a more integrative approach, there are several techniques to combine dreamwork with shamanic journeying. One method is to engage in shamanic drumming upon waking from a dream, using the rhythmic beats to re-enter the dream realm but with heightened lucidity, akin to a controlled shamanic journey. This allows for real-time interaction with dream elements and facilitates the extraction of deeper spiritual meanings.

Another technique is to practice "dream re-entry." Upon waking from a dream, instead of rising, stay in the liminal space between sleep and wakefulness and intentionally guide your consciousness back into the dream landscape. From there, you can explore the dream terrain with more agency, perhaps encountering spirits or guides as in a shamanic journey.

Yet another approach involves setting a "dream intention" before sleep, much like a shaman sets an intention before embarking on a journey. By focusing on a particular question or spiritual quest before sleep, you pave the way for dreams that are aligned with this intention. When these dreams occur, their symbolism and narrative can be interpreted as insights or answers to the quest, providing a unique blend of dream exploration and shamanic journeying.

In summary, the interplay between dreams and shamanic journeys offers a rich tapestry of experiences for those seeking spiritual wisdom and transformation. The dream realm's inherently otherworldly nature dovetails seamlessly with the shamanic concept of journeying between worlds, while the ritualistic and symbolic elements encountered in both states can serve as markers and tools for spiritual growth. Techniques that integrate both practices provide exciting avenues for deeper self-exploration and spiritual development.

CHAPTER 35: ARCHETYPAL PATTERNS AND COSMIC SYMBOLS

Introduction

As we venture further into the labyrinthine corridors of dreams and their symbolism, we arrive at a juncture where mere mortals brush shoulders with the transcendent. Here, we're no longer just dealing with common dream symbols like houses, roads, or even animals. Instead, we are entering a realm where the symbols in question are grander, often elusive, and resonate with the frequency of the cosmos itself. This chapter aims to unpack the enigma surrounding these archetypal patterns and cosmic symbols that occasionally but powerfully emerge in our dreamscapes.

The Role of Archetypes in Dream Symbols

Archetypes, as conceptualized primarily by Carl Jung, are primordial, universal ideas that reside in the collective unconscious. They are patterns or molds filled in with the particulars of experience in an individual's life. An archetype, such as "The Hero," "The Wise Old Man," or "The Great Mother," isn't just a figure in a narrative; it's a living psychic force that can manifest itself in myriad ways.

When archetypes appear in dreams, they usually do so with grandeur. They stand apart from the mundane symbols and command attention. Often they are richly detailed, uncanny, and evoke a sense of awe or fear. These archetypes can appear as characters, such as a sage, a temptress, or even a shape-shifting entity. They can also manifest as scenarios, like death and rebirth, cosmic conflict, or a return to paradise. The dreamer usually experiences a sense of being part of something larger than themselves, and the event often lingers in the memory long after waking up.

The purpose of these archetypal patterns in dreams often points to essential life lessons or existential concerns that need to be addressed. For example, if you find yourself guided by a Wise Old Man in your dreams, it might be an invitation to seek wisdom and guidance in your waking life, possibly indicating a phase of inward reflection and meditation.

Cosmic Symbols: A Language Beyond Language

While archetypes can be somewhat localized within the cultural or mythological context, cosmic symbols are even more enigmatic and universal. They could be seen as "high-order" archetypes that do not just dwell in the human collective unconscious but perhaps in the very fabric of the universe itself. These include symbols like the infinity loop, intricate fractals, and even sacred geometry like the Flower of Life. Such symbols often bear an intrinsic mathematical or geometric elegance, as if presenting a more profound equation that transcends human understanding.

When cosmic symbols appear in dreams, they often feel otherworldly, as if they carry messages from a realm far beyond our day-to-day reality. Encountering a cosmic symbol in a dream can be disorienting and awe-inspiring at the same time. These symbols don't readily offer a "meaning" in the way other dream symbols do. Instead, their impact is often visceral, affecting the dreamer at an emotional and spiritual level, often leaving them with more questions than answers.

Cosmic symbols could be seen as conduits of cosmic knowledge or wisdom, inviting the dreamer into a dialogue with the ineffable. They often encourage a form of spiritual awakening or, at the very least, a shift in perspective that considers the interconnectedness of all things. Such dreams could instigate deep spiritual inquiry or even inspire artistic endeavors aimed at encapsulating their intricate designs.

Integration and Transformation

Both archetypal patterns and cosmic symbols in dreams serve as profound gateways to self-knowledge and spiritual evolution. However, it's not sufficient merely to recognize them; one must integrate this awareness into daily life for transformation to occur. Encounters with archetypes might necessitate lifestyle changes or new paths in spiritual practices. In contrast, cosmic symbols often call for a restructuring of one's fundamental worldview.

A practical way to integrate these advanced dream symbols is through conscious reflection, meditation, and dialogue—either with a spiritual guide, a dream circle, or through journaling. Actively engaging with these symbols helps to ground their abstract nature into something more tangible, thereby allowing their transformative potential to unfold.

Summary

Archetypal patterns and cosmic symbols represent the zenith of mystical dream exploration. Far from the typical dream symbols that populate the average dream narrative, these are complex, richly textured manifestations from deep layers of the psyche and possibly beyond. Archetypes serve as essential life guides and cosmic symbols as dialogues with the ineffable, both requiring active integration to realize their full transformative potential. As we continue our journey through the realm of dreams, these mysterious symbols act like cosmic breadcrumbs, leading us ever closer to the ultimate realization of our interconnectedness with the vast, awe-inspiring universe.

CHAPTER 36: DREAM INTERPRETATION IN TRANSPERSONAL PSYCHOLOGY

Introduction

As we delve into the realm of advanced dream interpretation techniques, the field of transpersonal psychology offers profound insights. This psychological sub-discipline transcends the limits of traditional psychology by integrating spiritual experiences and states of altered consciousness, including dreams, into a broader understanding of human psyche. In this chapter, we will explore the advanced theories of dream interpretation in the context of transpersonal psychology, addressing how transpersonal theories extend our understanding beyond the egoic mind and into the realm of interconnectedness and higher states of being.

The Landscape of Transpersonal Psychology

Transpersonal psychology arose in the late 20th century, influenced by figures like Abraham Maslow, Carl Jung, and Stanislav Grof. Unlike traditional psychological paradigms that often focus solely on pathology or the egoic self, transpersonal psychology encompasses a fuller range of human experience, including peak experiences, mystical states, and spiritual emergencies. The overarching aim is to explore the deepest potentials of human consciousness, going beyond the individual to consider the transpersonal or "beyond-personal" aspects of the human psyche.

In dream interpretation, transpersonal psychology incorporates not just the personal unconscious, laden with memories, fears, and desires, but also the transpersonal unconscious, which connects to collective archetypes, cosmic wisdom, and perhaps even ancestral memories. This implies that some dreams may not just be reflective of individual concerns but may tap into a larger, interconnected web of universal consciousness.

Advanced Dream Interpretation Through Transpersonal Psychology

When applying the principles of transpersonal psychology to dream interpretation, several advanced techniques and perspectives come to light:

1. **Holotropic Dream Analysis**: Originated by Stanislav Grof, Holotropic Breathwork is a practice designed to evoke non-ordinary states of consciousness. The principles behind this can be applied to dream analysis, wherein the symbolism and emotional resonance of the dream are not just examined for personal meaning, but are also seen as gateways to broader, transpersonal insights.

2. **Spiritual Archetypes and Higher States**: While traditional psychological archetypes might include the Shadow or the Anima/Animus, in transpersonal psychology, archetypes can represent higher states of being or enlightenment. A dream featuring the archetype of "The Guru" or "The Mystic" might signify

not just a wise aspect of oneself but a genuine connection to spiritual wisdom.

3. **Past Life Resonances**: Some proponents of transpersonal psychology entertain the notion that certain dreams may be echoes of past life experiences. While empirically controversial, interpreting dreams through this lens may offer deep emotional and spiritual insights.

4. **Cosmic Consciousness**: Dreams of flying, outer space, or interconnected geometric patterns may be interpreted as tapping into a cosmic or universal mind, which is a frequent area of study in transpersonal psychology.

5. **Intersubjectivity and Shared Dreaming**: Transpersonal psychology allows for the exploration of the realm where the boundaries between the individual and others are blurred. The phenomena of shared dreams or dream telepathy can be more deeply understood by considering the transpersonal connections between individuals.

Through these methods and perspectives, dream interpretation in the realm of transpersonal psychology moves beyond mere self-exploration and opens up avenues for spiritual growth, interconnected understanding, and even cosmic awareness.

Critical Considerations

While transpersonal psychology offers fascinating avenues for dream interpretation, it is not without its critiques. The field has been criticized for its loose methodological approaches and its tendency to integrate concepts that are often deemed 'unscientific' like spirituality and mysticism. Therefore, while its insights can be profoundly transformative, they should be applied judiciously, and one should maintain a balanced perspective that incorporates both empirical evidence and subjective experience.

Summary

Transpersonal psychology enriches the domain of dream interpretation by offering a framework that transcends the individual and delves into realms of interconnectedness, spirituality, and higher states of consciousness. Its holistic approach incorporates both the personal and transpersonal aspects of human experience, allowing for a multifaceted understanding of dream symbolism and significance. However, as with any approach that integrates the metaphysical with the empirical, caution and discernment are advised. By navigating the intersection of dreams and transpersonal psychology, one can venture into the frontiers of human consciousness and perhaps gain glimpses into the cosmic fabric that weaves us all together.

CHAPTER 37: ANALYZING RECURRING DREAM THEMES

Introduction

Recurring dreams are a fascinating aspect of the dream landscape, offering rich material for analysis and spiritual development. These repetitive dream patterns can become an urgent language of the subconscious, highlighting unresolved issues or potentials for growth that demand attention. As we delve into the advanced level of understanding dreams, it's crucial to focus on the techniques for dissecting recurring dream themes. The purpose is not only to decode their meanings but also to integrate this understanding into our broader spiritual practice.

The Anatomy of Recurring Dreams

Recurring dreams differ from isolated dreams in several ways. They may appear over varying time spans—days, weeks, or even years—and may carry the same symbols, scenes, or emotional tones. Understanding their anatomy helps in decoding the messages intricately woven into the fabric of these dreams.

Temporal Consistency and Variations

One noteworthy aspect of recurring dreams is their temporal consistency. They can occur in distinct phases of one's life or may even span across several years, marking them as different from singular, context-dependent dreams. This persistence in timing often correlates with unresolved emotional or psychological states. For instance, recurring dreams of failing an exam might correspond to periods of high stress or a feeling of inadequacy in one's waking life.

Emotional and Symbolic Intensity

The emotional and symbolic content in recurring dreams is usually more intense than in non-recurring ones. The repetitive nature itself serves as an amplifier, magnifying the emotional tone and symbolic content. In the spiritual context, these intensified emotions and symbols act as clues to the deeper layers of the psyche that are requesting attention.

Complexity and Adaptability

Over time, recurring dreams can also adapt or evolve, incorporating new elements or shedding outdated ones. This dynamic quality offers a unique lens into one's evolving spiritual and psychological state. The progression or alteration in a recurring dream may indicate a partial resolution or a shift in understanding of the issues it encapsulates.

Techniques for Analyzing Recurring Dream Themes

Dissecting recurring dreams requires a multifaceted approach. The complexity of these dreams calls for more advanced techniques that combine introspective depth with analytical breadth.

Journaling with a Focus on Patterns

Advanced dream journaling, where patterns of recurring symbols or emotions are specifically marked and analyzed, can be particularly helpful. This differs from standard dream journaling by adding an extra layer of analytical categorization. It enables one to spot micro-variations between different instances of the same recurring dream, aiding in the identification of evolving elements within the recurring theme.

Active Imagination and Dialoguing

Carl Jung's technique of active imagination can be employed to engage with recurring dream elements. This involves entering a meditative state and then consciously interacting with the dream symbols as if they were independent entities. By dialoguing with these symbols, one can negotiate, question, and explore their roles, uncovering their significance in the realm of the spiritual unconscious.

Contemplative Integration

The goal of dissecting recurring dreams isn't merely intellectual understanding but spiritual integration. Thus, one might also engage in practices like mindfulness meditation, mantra repetition, or prayer, focusing on the decoded symbols or emotional states. These practices can help internalize the understanding, aligning it with one's broader spiritual goals.

Conclusion

Recurring dreams act as intricate tapestries woven from the threads of our deepest fears, desires, and potentials. Their repetitive nature serves both as a challenge and an opportunity. By using advanced journaling techniques, active imagination, and contemplative practices, one can not only decode the rich symbolism but also integrate these findings into a more holistic spiritual practice. Analyzing recurring dream themes thus provides a pathway for deeper self-understanding, psychological balance, and spiritual growth.

CHAPTER 38: DREAMS, DÉJÀ VU, AND ANOMALIES OF CONSCIOUSNESS

Dreams often inhabit the borderlands of our comprehension, tantalizing us with their mysteriousness and intriguing us with their potential for revealing deeper truths. Yet, there are certain phenomena that seem to exist even further on the periphery of understanding, defying easy explanation and challenging our preconceptions about the nature of reality and consciousness. This chapter aims to explore some of these enigmatic territories, particularly focusing on the relationship between dreams, déjà vu, and other anomalies of consciousness.

The Mystery of Déjà Vu

Déjà vu is a French term that translates to "already seen," and it is a psychological phenomenon where one feels that they have already experienced a current situation, even though they rationally know it's the first time they are encountering it. While most people experience déjà vu as a fleeting and curious oddity, its underpinnings suggest a tantalizing overlap with dreams. Both dreams and déjà vu incidents can be understood as disruptions or irregularities in memory processing and subjective time perception.

Several theories aim to explain déjà vu. Cognitive theories often attribute it to a glitch in memory retrieval, whereby a person misidentifies a novel experience as familiar. Other hypotheses link déjà vu to the interplay between the brain's neural circuits, where the neurons that transmit information about the present may overlap with the neurons storing past experiences. In the mystical or spiritual context, déjà vu has been linked to past lives, parallel universes, or the echoes of premonitions from dreams that have somehow embedded themselves into our subconscious.

The Dream Connection

Dreams can serve as a precursor to déjà vu in various ways. Some people report having dreamt of places or events that they later encounter in waking life, giving them an uncanny sensation of recognition. While such accounts are largely anecdotal and often fraught with the perils of selective memory and interpretation, they cannot be entirely dismissed. The Jungian concept of synchronicity, or meaningful coincidence, might offer a conceptual framework for understanding these phenomena. In this view, both dreams and déjà vu can be seen as part of a larger pattern of interconnectedness that defies conventional explanations grounded solely in cause and effect.

Other theories posit that dreams can serve as a rehearsal space for waking life events, an idea that finds some support in evolutionary psychology. According to this view, déjà vu could be a byproduct of these rehearsals, a cognitive echo of a scenario or experience that was first encountered in a dream state.

Anomalies of Consciousness

Beyond déjà vu, dreams intersect with a range of

other anomalous experiences that challenge conventional understandings of consciousness. Phenomena like precognitive dreams, out-of-body experiences, and lucid dreaming all point to a more complex, multi-layered reality than what is accessible through our ordinary waking consciousness. For example, precognitive dreams, in which future events are foreseen, disturb our linear understanding of time and causality, as do phenomena like retrocausality, which is explored in quantum physics.

Similarly, out-of-body experiences and astral projection, often reported in dream-like states, suggest the possibility of a non-localized consciousness that can perceive events from a viewpoint detached from the physical body. While these phenomena lack rigorous scientific explanation, they invite us to expand our understanding of what consciousness is and how it interacts with the fabric of reality.

Lucid dreaming, in which the dreamer becomes aware that they are dreaming, offers another intriguing entry point into the discussion. By mastering the ability to consciously navigate their dream landscape, lucid dreamers challenge the boundaries between the subconscious and conscious mind, suggesting a more fluid, interconnected relationship between different states of awareness.

In summary, the realm of dreams offers fertile ground for exploring various anomalies of consciousness, including déjà vu. While these phenomena remain elusive and often defy conventional scientific explanation, they hold the promise of expanding our understanding of reality, consciousness, and the intricate ways in which they are intertwined. Whether viewed through the lens of psychology, spirituality, or even quantum mechanics, these anomalies beckon us to widen the scope of what we consider possible, inviting us into deeper layers of understanding and experience.

CHAPTER 39: ACTIVATING THE THIRD EYE THROUGH DREAMWORK

In the realm of dreamwork and spirituality, the concept of the "third eye" stands as a critical node where intuition, foresight, and transcendental wisdom converge. Positioned metaphysically in the middle of the forehead, slightly above the space between the eyebrows, the third eye is often considered the seat of insight in various spiritual traditions. This chapter delves into advanced techniques to activate the third eye through dreamwork. With the groundwork laid in previous chapters on dream interpretation, lucid dreaming, and archetypal patterns, we now venture into the esoteric practice of stimulating the third eye to augment the richness and spiritual significance of our dreams.

Anatomical and Metaphysical Aspects of the Third Eye

To understand the intricate process of activating the third eye through dreamwork, one must appreciate its dual representation: anatomical and metaphysical. Anatomically, the third eye is often equated with the pineal gland, a small, pinecone-shaped gland situated deep within the human brain.

This gland is linked to the regulation of sleep-wake cycles and the production of melatonin, a hormone involved in sleep. It has been proposed that the pineal gland could also produce endogenous dimethyltryptamine (DMT), a compound that has powerful psychoactive effects, though this is still a subject of scientific debate.

Metaphysically, the third eye transcends its physiological counterpart. In Eastern spiritual traditions such as Hinduism and Buddhism, it is known as the "ajna" chakra, the sixth primary chakra, and is believed to be the gateway to higher states of consciousness. Opening the third eye is said to result in clairvoyance, heightened intuition, and even telepathy. Activating the third eye within the context of dreamwork thus presents an opportunity for transcendent experiences and a deeper understanding of one's unconscious dynamics.

Techniques for Third Eye Activation in Dreamwork

Third Eye Meditation Before Sleep

One of the most effective ways to activate the third eye in conjunction with dreamwork is through pre-sleep meditation focused specifically on the ajna chakra. This involves lying down in a comfortable position, closing your eyes, and directing your mental focus to the area slightly above and between your eyebrows. Envision an indigo light emanating from this point and expanding with each inhalation. As you exhale, imagine the light penetrating deeper into your forehead, illuminating the mind and priming it for spiritually significant dreams.

Lucid Dreaming and Third Eye Visualization

If you've mastered the art of becoming lucid in dreams—a skill discussed in previous chapters—you can take this opportunity to work on third eye activation within the dream state. Once lucid, visualize your third eye in the same way you would in waking meditation. Given that the dream state is already an altered form of consciousness, the act of third eye activation here can produce profoundly enlightening experiences.

Dream Journaling with Third Eye Awareness

Another technique involves the use of a dream journal, not just as a passive record but as an active tool for third eye activation. After waking from a dream, and while still in a liminal state between sleep and wakefulness, focus your awareness on your third eye as you recount and record the dream. This concentrated focus can act as a form of active meditation, enabling you to draw deeper insights from your dreams.

Potential Challenges and Ethical Considerations

Activating the third eye through dreamwork is a high-intensity spiritual practice that may not be suitable for everyone. Some people report experiencing overwhelming visions, emotional turbulence, or existential crises. Ethical considerations also come into play, especially in dealing with newfound intuitive or clairvoyant abilities. It is crucial to approach this practice with humility and a sense of responsibility, understanding that the opening of the third eye is not an end but a beginning—the inauguration of a deeper commitment to spiritual growth and self-understanding.

In summary, the activation of the third eye through dreamwork is an advanced practice that blends anatomical understanding with metaphysical insights. Techniques such as focused pre-sleep meditation, in-dream visualizations, and post-dream journaling can serve as effective tools in this endeavor. However, this practice is not without its challenges and ethical quandaries, demanding a responsible approach. Mastering the activation of the third eye can pave the way for an enriched tapestry of dream experiences and a more profound engagement with the spiritual dimensions of existence.

CHAPTER 40: SACRED DREAM CIRCLES: COLLECTIVE DREAM INTERPRETATION

Dream interpretation is often seen as a solitary endeavor. However, the collective experience of dream analysis can offer unique insights and deepen the understanding of dream symbolism. In spiritual traditions across various cultures, dream circles—gatherings where participants openly discuss their dreams in a structured, supportive environment—have been used for this purpose. This chapter delves into the formation and effective utilization of sacred dream circles for collective insight and interpretation.

The Concept and Origins of Dream Circles

Dream circles have roots in many spiritual traditions, from Native American cultures to certain schools of Buddhism. They function on the principle that a collective wisdom can emerge from a group of individuals engaged in sincere dialogue. In other words, the sum can be greater than its parts. Traditionally, these circles were not only a means for interpreting dreams but also a way to connect deeply with the community and its shared spirituality. They could serve as an open forum for communal guidance, as well as for transmitting esoteric knowledge. Participants often found that the act of articulating dreams, and hearing them vocalized by others, allowed for an emergent, often surprising, understanding of the symbolic language of dreams.

In the modern context, dream circles can also be a part of psychotherapeutic practices, often merging with Jungian or transpersonal psychology techniques. Participants are encouraged to view the dream from multiple angles—cultural, archetypal, personal, and collective. The circles can be either physical gatherings or online meetings, although the former is generally preferred for its ability to foster a sense of sacredness and shared space.

Structural Elements of a Dream Circle

Forming and conducting a dream circle requires careful planning and adherence to certain structural elements to maintain its sacred integrity. Below are key components:

1. **Selection of Participants**: Care must be taken to select participants who are genuinely interested in engaging with the dreamwork. This ensures that the energy of the circle remains focused and elevated.

2. **Setting the Intent**: At the beginning of each meeting, a clear intention should be stated. This could range from understanding specific symbols to broader goals like enhancing spiritual awareness.

3. **Safe and Sacred Space**: It's imperative to establish a safe, non-judgmental environment. Many traditions involve setting up an altar or using certain ritualistic elements to sanctify the space.

4. **Structured Sharing**: One person at a time shares a dream while others listen attentively. The individual

sharing should not be interrupted during this time.

5. **Collective Analysis**: After a dream has been shared, participants offer their interpretations, always reminding that each interpretation is subjective. Often a 'talking stick' is passed around to designate who has the floor for speaking, maintaining order and respect within the circle.

Integrating Collective Wisdom into Individual Dreamwork

One of the fascinating aspects of dream circles is the potential to integrate collective insights into one's personal dreamwork. Hearing varied interpretations often uncovers facets of the dream that may not have been apparent in solitary analysis. This provides a broader and richer understanding of one's dreams and their implications.

Furthermore, dream circles often report episodes of synchronicity—meaningful coincidences that resonate deeply with participants, such as recurring themes or symbols across different individual dreams. These synchronicities can serve as powerful affirmations of the circle's collective intention or focus.

Participants are encouraged to maintain their own dream journals and incorporate insights gained from the circle into their own personal dreamwork regimen. This could mean revisiting a dream with new perspectives or even incubating dreams with questions or themes that emerged from the circle. Additionally, integrating these collective insights can extend to other spiritual practices like meditation or ritual work, making the dream circle not merely an isolated event but part of a greater tapestry of spiritual growth.

Summary

Dream circles offer a collective approach to dream interpretation, deeply rooted in various cultural and spiritual traditions. The circle serves as both a forum for shared wisdom and a sacred space for individual exploration. Through careful selection of participants, clear intent, and structured sharing, these circles can be an enriching extension of individual dreamwork. By weaving in collective insights, not only can one achieve a more nuanced understanding of their dreams, but it can also serve as a springboard for broader spiritual exploration and growth.

CHAPTER 41: EROTIC DREAMS AND SPIRITUAL ALCHEMY

Introduction

The subject of erotic dreams is often fraught with confusion and discomfort, especially when these dreams intersect with our spiritual journey. Nevertheless, erotic dreams hold the potential to be catalysts for profound transformation. This chapter explores the landscape of erotic dreams within the realm of spiritual alchemy. It aims to provide a nuanced understanding of how these dreams can be considered as important markers and transformative agents in one's spiritual growth.

The Spectrum of Erotic Dreams

Erotic dreams can span a broad spectrum, from subtle, romantic encounters to explicit sexual situations. It's crucial to differentiate between the types and degrees of eroticism that can manifest in dreams to have a nuanced understanding of their significance. Broadly, erotic dreams can be categorized into:

- Platonic Connections: Dreams where the emphasis is on a deep emotional connection rather than explicit sexual content. These dreams often involve soulful conversations, holding hands, or deep eye contact.

- Sexual Encounters: Dreams that involve explicit sexual situations or activities. These dreams may also include fetishes, fantasies, or other unconventional expressions of sexuality.
- Romantic Encounters: These dreams combine elements of both platonic and sexual experiences, focusing on the emotional intimacy that accompanies physical attraction.

Symbolism and Alchemical Transformation

Erotic dreams are not mere expressions of repressed desires or biological drives. In the context of spiritual alchemy, the process by which base instincts are transmuted into higher spiritual values, erotic dreams offer fertile ground for transformation. Several alchemical symbols and processes can elucidate the transformative power of eroticism in dreams.

1. **Solve et Coagula**: This Latin term is a cornerstone of alchemical philosophy, translating to "dissolve and coagulate." In erotic dreams, dissolution might manifest as the breaking down of ego boundaries through intimacy, while coagulation signifies the forging of a new, more holistic self.
2. **Coniunctio**: This is the alchemical marriage, the union of opposites. Erotic dreams often feature elements of duality—masculine and feminine, submission and domination, love and lust—that seek integration.
3. **Nigredo, Albedo, Rubedo**: These are the stages of alchemical transformation—blackening, whitening, and reddening, respectively. Erotic dreams can take us through these stages by initially confronting us with our shadow selves (Nigredo), then purifying our

intentions (Albedo), and finally leading to a renewed sense of wholeness and integration (Rubedo).

Ethical and Practical Implications

Understanding the spiritual significance of erotic dreams brings about a need for ethical responsibility. Such dreams should not be taken as endorsements to act out any inappropriate or harmful fantasies in the real world, particularly if they involve non-consenting parties. They must be approached with maturity, insight, and a willingness to confront uncomfortable truths about oneself.

Dream journals can be an invaluable resource for decoding the messages in erotic dreams. Noting down the symbols, settings, and emotions associated with these dreams can help in identifying recurring patterns and themes. Over time, this allows for a more insightful and nuanced understanding, aiding the process of spiritual alchemy.

Summary

Erotic dreams hold a unique place in the tapestry of our nocturnal experiences. They challenge us, confront us with our deepest desires and fears, and offer avenues for transformative spiritual work. Through the lens of spiritual alchemy, we can view these dreams as intricate puzzles that, when decoded, provide keys to deeper spiritual insight and transformation. When handled with ethical awareness and practical wisdom, erotic dreams can be integrated meaningfully into one's broader spiritual practice.

CHAPTER 42: DREAM MAPPING: ADVANCED SYMBOL NETWORKS

Introduction

As we traverse the expansive world of dream interpretation, we arrive at a sophisticated technique known as "Dream Mapping." This advanced method requires a foundational understanding of dream symbols, archetypes, and a myriad of interpretation techniques previously discussed. Dream Mapping allows us to unravel the intricate web of interconnected dream symbols and their meanings, giving us a more comprehensive insight into the multilayered messages of our dreams. By constructing symbol networks, we can detect patterns, relationships, and even paradoxical elements that may otherwise go unnoticed.

Symbol Networks and the Cognitive Map

Understanding a single dream symbol can be likened to dissecting a word in a sentence. While you get the meaning of that particular word, you might miss its role in the overall context. A symbol network, on the other hand, takes into account the relationship between various dream symbols and contextualizes them within the broader tapestry of your dream world.

In cognitive psychology, a "cognitive map" refers to a mental representation of spatial relations between objects in one's environment. When we talk about Symbol Networks in the context of dreams, we are essentially talking about constructing a 'cognitive map' of our dream environment. This allows us to look beyond isolated symbols and dive deeper into the intricate interrelationships between them, which might include dualities, hierarchies, or even symbiotic relationships.

To construct this map, you would list out the main symbols in your dream and try to establish connections between them. For example, if you dreamt about a river crossing, a forest, and a key, you would not only interpret these symbols individually but also explore how they relate to each other. Does the river symbolize an emotional barrier you're trying to cross? Could the forest represent the unknown that you will encounter once you cross? And does the key signify a solution or insight that will assist you in navigating this unknown territory?

Techniques for Advanced Dream Mapping

Interconnected Symbol Analysis

One technique in Dream Mapping involves identifying and analyzing symbols that appear interconnected or repetitive across multiple dreams. Here, we are not just looking for recurring symbols, but symbols that appear in various forms and contexts yet bear a common thread. For instance, you may dream of climbing a mountain one night and ascending a ladder the next. Although the symbols are different, the underlying theme of 'ascension' or 'overcoming challenges' might be constant.

Contextual Symbol Evaluation

Another technique in Dream Mapping is the evaluation of symbols within various contexts. For example, water may symbolize emotions when appearing as a calm lake but might indicate danger or fear when seen as a turbulent ocean. By creating a context-specific mapping, you can evaluate how the meanings of individual symbols evolve or shift based on their context. This can offer a more nuanced interpretation that respects the complexity and fluidity of the dream landscape.

Synergistic Symbol Interpretation

A synergistic approach to Dream Mapping considers the combined impact of interconnected symbols. For example, dreaming of a snake in a garden may conjure biblical undertones of temptation and knowledge. However, when accompanied by other symbols like a crescent moon or a chalice, the snake could take on a more transformative or feminine connotation, as in alchemical symbolism.

Summary

Dream Mapping is not a linear process but rather an evolving practice that adapts as you continue your journey into the dream world. This advanced technique of creating symbol networks adds another layer of depth to dream interpretation by exploring the interrelationships between different symbols. Whether you are employing interconnected symbol analysis, contextual symbol evaluation, or a synergistic approach, Dream Mapping offers a multi-faceted, holistic avenue for understanding the complex narratives that unfold in the dreamscape. Through this practice, we can better integrate dream wisdom into our waking consciousness, enriching both our spiritual and psychological lives.

CHAPTER 43: TRANSCENDING THE SELF: NON-DUAL AWARENESS IN DREAMING

Introduction

As we delve into the advanced terrains of dream analysis, one of the profound notions that emerge is the idea of non-dual awareness. This concept challenges our ordinary, dualistic way of perceiving the world and ourselves, offering instead a unified field of experience that transcends individual ego and even the apparent separation between dreamer and dream. The purpose of this chapter is to elaborate on advanced practices for achieving non-dual awareness within the dreaming state, elucidating how this state of consciousness can enrich both our dreamwork and spiritual practice.

The Concept of Non-Dual Awareness

Non-dual awareness or non-duality is a term that finds its origins in various spiritual and philosophical traditions, notably in Vedanta, Taoism, and certain schools of Buddhist thought. It refers to a state of consciousness where the subject-object dichotomy dissolves, leading to a direct experience of reality as a unified whole. In this state, one transcends the limitations of ego and individuality, recognizing the interconnectedness of all phenomena. Such an awareness can offer profoundly transformative experiences, yet it is often deemed elusive, indescribable, or paradoxical.

In the context of dreaming, non-dual awareness implies a kind of transcendent lucidity that goes beyond merely being aware that one is dreaming. It encapsulates the dissolution of barriers not only between the dreamer and the dream but also among the various elements within the dream. This results in an experience that is imbued with a deep sense of oneness, absence of judgment, and a form of 'knowing' that transcends intellectual understanding.

Practices for Achieving Non-Dual Awareness in Dreams

Dreamwork that focuses on non-dual awareness often incorporates meditation techniques, practices to cultivate mindfulness, and methods adapted from non-dual traditions.

Mindfulness Meditation

Integrating mindfulness meditation into your pre-sleep routine can help you become an observer of your thoughts, emotions, and bodily sensations without judgment. This form of detached observation is a step towards experiencing non-duality, as it helps diminish the subject-object distinction. Practice mindfulness as you drift to sleep with the intention of carrying this awareness into your dreams.

Dream Yoga

Derived from Tibetan Buddhism, dream yoga practices offer direct techniques to cultivate non-dual awareness within the dreaming state. These practices often involve exercises to maintain awareness as you transition from wakefulness to sleep and vice versa. Skilled practitioners claim to reach states of pure, non-conceptual awareness within the dream, echoing non-dualistic experiences.

Direct Inquiry

Some practitioners employ methods of self-inquiry within the dream state. This involves asking questions like, "Who is dreaming?" or "What is the nature of this dream experience?" Such inquiry can lead to a collapse of the dream ego and a consequent realization of non-dual awareness.

The Implications of Non-Dual Awareness in Dreaming for Spiritual Practice

Achieving a state of non-dual awareness within dreams has far-reaching implications for spiritual practice. It provides a direct experiential understanding of complex philosophical and spiritual principles, allowing for their easier integration into waking life. This state of awareness serves as a potent reminder of the impermanent, interdependent nature of all phenomena, encouraging a holistic, compassionate worldview.

Moreover, non-dual awareness in dreaming offers a form of cognitive and spiritual liberation. By overcoming the inherent dualities that constrain our understanding—such as good versus bad, self versus other, and even dream versus reality—we unlock a level of freedom and peace that can permeate all aspects of life.

Summary

Non-dual awareness in dreaming offers a transformative state of consciousness that dissolves the barriers of ego and duality, encouraging a unified field of experience. Achieving this state requires specialized practices such as mindfulness meditation, dream yoga, and direct inquiry. The realization of non-dual awareness within dreams can have profound implications for spiritual practices, enriching our understanding of interconnectedness, and providing a palpable sense of cognitive and spiritual liberation. This advanced level of dreamwork stands as a potent frontier in the integration of dream analysis and spiritual growth.

CHAPTER 44: INTEGRATING DREAM WISDOM INTO DAILY SPIRITUAL PRACTICE

In this penultimate chapter, we delve into the intricate yet compelling task of integrating the wisdom acquired through dreamwork into your daily spiritual practices. As we've navigated through the labyrinthine world of dream symbols, archetypes, and mystical experiences, we've amassed a considerable toolkit for understanding our dreams. The challenge now is to make this abstract knowledge actionable, to bring it down from the ether of dreamscapes into the tangible routines of everyday life.

Seamless Integration: From Abstract to Actionable

One of the key obstacles people face is that dream insights often remain isolated from waking consciousness, secluded in the confines of a dream journal or vaguely recalled during occasional reflective moments. Yet, true spiritual transformation necessitates a more dynamic interplay between these separate states of consciousness. To accomplish this, consider creating a 'Dream Integration Journal,' separate from your regular dream journal, where you specifically note down actionable insights. For instance, if a recurring dream highlights a specific fear, you could devise a spiritual or psychological exercise to work on facing that fear.

This actionable component could be anything from engaging in focused meditation to practicing a particular yoga asana, or even invoking specific mantras or prayers that correlate with the dream's subject matter. The objective is to select practices that resonate with the dream's themes or messages and incorporate them into your existing daily spiritual routines. These practices serve as anchors, pulling the ethereal messages from your dreams into the realm of material action.

Esoteric Rituals and Dream Symbols

In many mystical traditions, from Hermeticism to Kabbalah, esoteric rituals hold a special place. These rituals often utilize complex symbols, words of power, and ritualistic actions to achieve specific spiritual goals. The dream world is replete with symbols that can be equally potent when employed in such rituals.

To integrate these, one could start by identifying key symbols or archetypes from recent dreams. These could be animals, geometric shapes, or even entire landscapes. Once identified, study the traditional meaning of these symbols within your chosen spiritual path, and integrate them into your rituals. For instance, if a serpent frequently appears in your dreams, and you are practicing Kundalini yoga, you might incorporate serpent imagery into your meditation visualizations to stimulate the rise of Kundalini energy. Alternatively, a dream symbol that corresponds to a specific Tarot card could be used in daily Tarot meditations.

Mindfulness as an Integrative Mechanism

Mindfulness, or the state of active, open attention on the present, provides a fertile ground for the integration of dream wisdom. This may seem counterintuitive since dreams are often considered the antithesis of waking, rational consciousness. However, the dream state and mindfulness share a common trait—they both invite a heightened awareness of the inner self.

By practicing mindfulness, especially during activities that resonate with dream symbols or messages, you create a seamless flow of spiritual wisdom between the dreaming and waking states. If your dreams have emphasized the importance of self-love, for instance, being mindfully present during self-care routines can serve to embed this dream wisdom more deeply into your psyche. Mindfulness acts as the bridge between the ephemeral world of dreams and the concrete world of daily action, enabling you to live your spiritual truths in a fully integrated manner.

Summary

To bring the profound insights from dreamwork into your everyday spiritual practice, it's essential to translate these often abstract understandings into actionable tasks. By creating a 'Dream Integration Journal,' incorporating dream symbols into esoteric rituals, and employing mindfulness as a mechanism for integration, you can achieve a harmonious interplay between dream wisdom and daily spirituality. By committing to these practices, you enrich not only your spiritual path but also deepen your understanding of the multi-dimensional self. This, in turn, fuels your dreamwork, creating a self-reinforcing loop of spiritual growth and awareness. Thus, the boundaries between dreamwork and daily spiritual practice start to blur, leading to a more unified and holistic approach to spiritual development.

CHAPTER 45: A POSITIVE FAREWELL: THE INFINITE POSSIBILITIES OF DREAMWORK

The Journey So Far

As we conclude our comprehensive voyage through the vast and intricate realm of dream interpretation and dreamwork, let's take a moment to acknowledge the layers of complexity and the wellsprings of insight that this study opens up for us. From the history and psychology of dreaming to the sophisticated spiritual practices that integrate dreamwork, you have now been armed with an extensive toolkit. This toolkit isn't just for dissecting the labyrinthine corridors of your dream world; it is also a vessel for your personal and spiritual growth.

The Endless Horizon of Dreamwork

The ending of this book is merely the prologue of your ongoing journey into the world of dreams. Each dream you experience offers an opportunity for deepening your understanding, enriching your spiritual practices, and guiding your everyday life. You've learned to read the universal language of dreams, discern the archetypes, and unravel the skein of symbols. You've also investigated the connection between dreams and altered states of consciousness, time perception, and quantum mechanics. Your dreams are an uncharted territory that can become an integral part of your daily spiritual practice, offering you perpetual avenues for self-discovery and enlightenment.

Incorporating dreamwork into your spiritual routines creates a synergetic effect. Just as your dreams can be better understood in the context of your spiritual beliefs and practices, so can your waking spirituality be profoundly enriched by the insights gained from your dreams. And this relationship is not static; it evolves. As you grow, mature, and undergo life changes, your dream symbols and themes will adapt, offering new layers of meaning and guidance. This constant evolution ensures that dreamwork never becomes a stagnant pool but remains a flowing river, perpetually refreshing and renewing your spiritual life.

The Limitless Canvas of Personal Transformation

What you've learned in this book is not just theoretical knowledge. It's an experiential curriculum, designed to be applied, adapted, and personalized. Whether you're keeping a dream journal or participating in a dream circle, you're engaging in a transformative process. Every dream you analyze and every symbol you decode serves as a brushstroke on the vast canvas of your spiritual life. Some of those strokes might represent moments of joy and realization, while others might signify trials and tribulations. But each one is essential in creating the masterpiece that is you.

Given the expansive possibilities of dreamwork, there is no end to how much you can grow and transform. The knowledge you've gained serves as a solid foundation, but the structure you build upon it is limited only by your imagination and commitment. And this is perhaps the most liberating aspect of dreamwork: its limitless nature. In the dream realm, you can be anyone, do anything, and go anywhere. By learning to navigate this inner cosmos, you open the door to infinite possibilities, not just in your dreams, but in your waking life as well.

In Summary

As we close this chapter and the book, take with you the understanding that the realm of dreamwork is a land of endless potential and infinite possibilities. It's a landscape where the mystical and the practical, the divine and the earthly, come together in a harmonious dance. As you continue to journey through this awe-inspiring terrain, remember that each dream is a new adventure, each symbol a clue, each interpretation a step closer to your higher self.

Dreamwork is not just a field of study but a way of life, a path that leads to deeper self-awareness and spiritual enlightenment. You've already taken the first steps on this exciting, endless path. May your journey be filled with wonder, wisdom, and an ever-deepening connection to the spiritual essence that is you.

THE END

Printed in Great Britain
by Amazon